THE 24TH SON

My Story of Survival and Sacrifice
in Sierra Leone's Civil War

Born three years before the brutal civil war broke out
in Sierra Leone, Ibrahim and his 23 siblings grew
up amongst the daily heavy choices of what and who
must be sacrificed to survive.

Ibrahim Bangura

Publication Date: 26 January 2023

NATIONAL LIBRARY OF AUSTRALIA

A catalogue record for this book is available from the National Library of Australia

———— 66 ————

"THERE IS ALWAYS A WAY.

I FOUND MY WAY.

YOU CAN FIND YOURS TOO"

———— 99 ————

FAMILY TREE

The 24th Son Ibrahim

Musa (23)

Issa (22)

RiRi (21)

Khalid (20)

Thaimu (19)

Miscarriage (18)

Isabella (16)

Abdul (P-to-P) (17)

Baida (14)

Sidu (15)

Haji (12)

Miscarriage (13)

Terriza (10)

Diamond (11)

Mabinty (9)

My Mother

Elder Mama

Father

Sheik (8)

Alus (6)

Cynthia (5)

Salamatu (7)

Sata (2)

Hass (1)

Abbigail (3)

Miscarriage (4)

Table of Contents

Introduction

"Shhh, be quiet. Do not make a sound."

"But Mama, I–"

"No! Not a word..."

I took one quick glance at her eyes. I could sense it. The fear. It was evident from the way her hands clutched mine so tightly, and how she spoke in hushed tones as we crouched low, flat on our bellies.

Whatever was causing this, I wanted it to end quickly. I was already becoming restless. I had made plans the previous day and was itching to get started.

Boom!

The loud noise jolted me out of my daydream. My mother's hands wrapped around mine even tighter.

"Mama, wh–wha–what is...?" I felt the first shiver of fear run down my spine.

"Listen to me, my son." Her beautiful, round eyes were moist with tears. "Listen and do as I say. We have to survive! We must."

Little did I know that, from then on, my carefree, happy childhood was over.

Everyone has scars. Everyone has fears. But not everyone grew up in a time when it was common to see bodies piled on the streets. Not everyone comes from a family of 24 children. As children, we had to duck in the bushes to avoid bullets from enemy soldiers. We constantly had to choose between what—and who—to sacrifice in order to survive.

You see, I grew up during a brutal civil war. This terrible civil war plagued the country I called home for 11 years: Sierra Leone.

This is my story. This is my voice. The voice of both a child and a man. A child forced to end his childhood in order to survive. A child who went through the trauma of a civil war and learned about loss and death before he could spell. A man who survived the 11-year-long war and found refuge in Australia. A man whose dreams are still haunted by memories of the war. This story is about this life motto: Even in the hardest times, you can choose to see things positively.

I have achieved my three goals—getting degree, having a wife, and buying a house—and was even lucky enough to have my beloved mother there to witness it all. But will it all come undone because of the legacy of the war?

Like every survivor, I owe it to myself to share my story. My mothers and siblings have yet to share their stories, but this is mine... I am bringing my story to you. If you had 23 siblings, how would you begin your story? Let me take you to the place where it all began...

CHAPTER 1

My Mother's Coming of Age

My father had two wives. My mother had 12 children, and my stepmother had 12 children (including two sets of twins). I am child number 24.

I do not think anyone planned for our family to be this big. I could use all capital letters for BIG, because having 24 children is no joke. But this wasn't anything too strange in my hometown. Families were far more extended than nuclear. Having children was seen as a display of fertility, strength, or wealth. Poverty played a huge role in the ignorance and lack of development of my people. When my mother was young, as well as when I was young, there was little to no education and restricted access to medical supplies and basic living necessities. I was inseparable from my brother, Musa; he was also my best friend, and the 23rd child. He had an illness that could have easily been controlled by medication, but in Sierra Leone at that time, his condition was associated with the work of the devil. In hard times like this, the light at the end of the tunnel is blurry.

My mother got married *'wae e pull borbi'*, which translates to 'when she hit puberty' or 'when her boobs matured'. I'm guessing she was around 14 when this happened. People didn't know their exact date of birth then. In most cases, parents would associate significant milestones in their lives, such as deaths and birthdays, with seasons and memorable occasions. They would often tell their child, 'You were born in the year we had so much rain' or 'when your father had the biggest return on his farm'. Either of these could mean that you were born on any date from June to November, which was our rainy season. If you happened to be born in the dry season, they would say something like: 'You were born the year the bush downtown was burned and when people caught a lot of animals'. Sometimes, you would even hear my people say, 'You were born a few days after your uncle's daughter was born' with no specific dates. That was it!

The only people who knew and cared about their date of birth were the rich people in the city who were fortunate enough to afford the luxuries of life.

My father was already a full-grown man when my mother was offered to him in marriage. How old was he exactly? I do not know, and neither does my mother. In those days, nobody bothered with such things.

Marriage, though, was something entirely different. It was serious business for my people and was conducted with due diligence and obedience to the culture. I have now come to see it as an unnecessary action. You see, in most parts of Sierra Leone, parents and other close family relatives in charge of a girl or a woman felt it was their responsibility to marry their daughter to a good man from their perspective and judgment. Due to this ideology, it became the standard practice for caregivers to pick a man they deemed fit and to ask them if they would be interested in marrying their daughters. In most cases, especially for women from poor socio-economic backgrounds, they were the barter for how families reconnected, how feuds were settled, and how commerce was exchanged.

The girls had no say. The decisions were made on their behalf, and all they could do was accept it or risk becoming outcasts. It was a scary thing to be cast off by one's family and almost none of the girls dared to take this route.

This is precisely what happened to my mother. When my father visited my mother's village, my grandmother and elder aunty decided they would make a judgment on whether my father would be a suitable candidate for my mother—without her input, of course. Within a few minutes, he had impressed them enough for them to ask him to marry my mother. All this was decided while my mother was at the stream fetching water. When she returned home, she was instructed to go and say hello to the stranger outside.

"You see that man?" my aunty began. "He will be your husband and you will be his wife. You are going to marry him."

That was it. No consultation. No opinion. Her fate had already been decided.

On a cloudy winter day in June 2021, my mother had a conversation with me that recounted the events that followed this visit. She told me that she had spent the first night in tears, thinking, *How could they give me away to such a poor old man?*

My mother explained that she was inconsolable as she weighed her options. There were only two things she could do: stand her ground and refuse to marry the old stranger (and face the shame and disgrace it would bring), or give up on any opinions she had and simply go along with the cultural expectations.

My mother clarified that she obviously chose the latter. This stranger would later be called my father—

the man who would play such a major role in both my mother's life and mine. She continued revealing her story to me, and I will now share it with you.

My father returned to his village, Madina, and my mother's training for married life began. Every day, my grandmother and aunty would teach her how to cook and serve her husband's food. The rice had to be put in a separate bowl and moulded into a hill-looking shape. To do this, you had to fill three-quarters of the bowl with cooked rice and dip the wooden cooking spatula into a bowl of water. The mixture was next turned in a circular motion. This required concentration and precision to turn out as it should, and the older women made sure my mother perfected every step. The sweet green potato leaves, cassava leaves, or soup sauce had to be placed in another bowl. Mixing the rice and sauce in one bowl was not allowed. The husband was to have the best part of any meat she cooked. She was earnestly informed that this was extremely important.

My people treasured good food, and a woman who knew how to cook was a high prize and held a straight ticket to her husband's affections.

Although my mother's lessons in the kitchen was over, her overall training was far from finished. The next lesson was teaching my mother about sex. For this, there is only one rule: *never* refuse sex when your husband asks. Her husband was the owner of her body, and she was to ensure she granted him pleasure at all times.

Even though I was not born yet, I am imagining nothing about my mother's opinions was taken into consideration, and no other feminine knowledge regarding sexual health or care was passed down. After all, my grandmother and aunty could only pass down what they knew, and that was exactly what they did.

By the end of their training, my mother was deemed ready to be taken to her husband's home. She now knew how to cook, clean, serve her husband and never refuse him sex. That was all she needed. Or so they thought.

Soon, it was time for the rites that would send my mother off to her matrimonial home. On the same day, the famous harmattan wind blew from the Sahara. This brought humidity and the temperature dropped until it was almost too cold for the locals. My grandmother was in charge of the ceremony. She organised the ceremonial package, which comprised of a calabash, a mat, bitter cola and a needle and thread, all wrapped in white cloth. All these items signified something essential about marriage.

The calabash was a hard shell of fruit from the gourd family. In Sierra Leone, several aspects of human livelihood and activities like food processing, cooking, fishing, hunting, and music, to name a few, were all facilitated by a different specific calabash. In a wedding, the calabash represented the expectation that the woman would be as efficient as the calabash.

The mat represented a comfortable place to sit with one's husband. To some, this signified making the house a home. Bitter cola or cola nuts represented that married life was not always sweet and there were going to be some unpleasant moments.

The needle and thread represented the saying: 'For every successful man, there is a woman behind him'. So, this expressed the expectation of the woman to stitch together the relationship.

The white cloth represented the expectation for the woman to be a virgin.

Three days after my mother was taken to the man, who had now become her husband, my grandmother sat on the doorsteps of her two-bedroom, clay and palm tree house, deep in thought.

Wearing nothing but a bright-coloured, two-yard *lappa*—the traditional clothing of woman from Sierra Leone—knotted just underneath her armpit in the cold harmattan morning, she kept sweating as her brain processed one thought after another. She kept her eyes fixed on the one-foot-wide narrow path that was framed by tall, dry grass. It led into the town from the big mountain forest; a one-meter-deep freshwater stream ran across the path, 100 meters from the mountains. She waited every morning, tense with anticipation I am imagining.

She did not have to wait for long. Finally, a young man surged from the mountain and brought the news to my grandma, who had been in agony for days. She gathered the elders of the village, and everyone sat anxiously.

With gleaming eyes, the young man exclaimed to my grandmother, "Marie, your daughter has made you all proud. She was a virgin!"

The crowd erupted with applause. The young man presented the white cloth that was used on the bed where my father had first lain with my mother, along with cola nuts and money as a sign of appreciation.

My grandmother was a farmer. She had about 50 goats, 60 sheep and 30 cows. While the young boys were mobilising for the evening celebration, Grandmother quickly grabbed an old, bright-coloured, dirty lappa and sandals made from old tyres.

Tyres … When my mother said this, it brought back fond memories. A story of my uncles finding tyres.

Once a year or so, while my uncles were walking from sunrise to sunset to visit family relatives in the other villages, they would sometimes be lucky enough to stumble upon old tyres. Treating it like a treasure, they would each carry one on their heads for 12 hours, walking under extreme weather—around 30 degrees

Celsius—back home to Sendoku.

The old tyres were so scarce that when people found them, their initial thought was about how to use them efficiently. To make sandals, they would first mark the family member's traces with a medium foot size, not the smallest or biggest. They would then cut the old tyres using a small, sharp knife made by the local blacksmith and hit nails with a hammer to hold the strips together.

This way, the whole family could share a few pairs throughout the year with the unisex, medium size.

There was no two ways about it. The family members with bigger shoe sizes learned to squeeze their feet into the medium sandals, while those with smaller shoe sizes had their feet practically swimming in the sandals. Fortunately, my mother was medium-sized, so the situation was always in her favour. She told me. The most important thing was that the shoes were not empty.

As soon as she was done strapping the buckles, Grandmother began her hour-long trek to her farm. There, she sought the finest two-year-old Texas longhorn cow. These cows were known for their characteristic horns, sometimes growing over 69 inches, and measuring up to 100 inches from tip to tip for steers and exceptional cows. This particular cow was full of energy—the perfect kill for such an occasion.

Grandmother tied the most durable rope she could find onto the female cow's longhorns and wrestled with it for the hour walk back home. Her goal? To give it to the young man who had brought the news so that he could take it back to my father and mother as a gift.

The young man would have to walk several miles back home to the people who had sent him on this journey and bring with him a heavy gift. But his face was beaming with pride I'll imagined. The distance was not of any matter to him.

He was honoured to have been chosen to deliver this news and to return to his village with such a significant gift. The elders had entrusted him with this task, and it was a source of pride for him.

The young man was asked to stay the night and to begin his journey when the rooster crowed. This crowing was the alarm clock for people in the village and from what I came to learn from my mother, this crowing usually began around 5 am.

You would think my grandmother's gift of such a big cow was the height of the celebration, but far from it. The young man who came as a messenger was to be properly treated, too. And for him, my grandmother organised one of the biggest roosters to be killed and cooked. With this meat, she would prepare her specialty: peanut soup.

As I reminisce now, I think of how my grandmother made the best peanut soup groundnut soup!

The night that she cooked for the messenger, the young man, she used peanut paste, fresh chilies, onions, salt, and fresh tomatoes. Of course, the rooster meat was added to complete the combo.

The peanut paste was made of raw peanuts roasted in a medium-hot pan until they were nicely browned. White Maggie (seasoning cubes) were then added along with salt and dried fish, then everything was pounded together. The peanut paste and the rest of the ingredients were finally mixed and cooked diligently on the fire stones.

The fire stones were used as a cooking stove and were made up of three big stones placed together in a circular shape. Then, dry wood was positioned in three directions to meet in the centre of the rocks. Fire was then ignited where the wood met, and the pot was placed on top.

Once this was done, the cooking began. It was cooked using the typical African style—one that continues to this day.

Grandmother always started by first frying a combination of the ingredients in freshly made palm oil. The smell ... Ahh...You could smell it from the other side of the world!

And it tasted even better than it smelled. Arguably, she made the best peanut soup in the whole three kingdoms. When she finished cooking, she would dish out six different bowls to share with three neighbours to the right and three neighbours to the left. This was a known tradition for generations.

The sky was beautiful the night that Grandmother

made her soup for the messenger. The village was lit up with a red sunset. The active, hardworking, powerful, and finest young men in the town were perfecting their Bubu instruments. Bubu is traditional music played by the Temne tribe from the north and west of Sierra Leone. I'm from this tribe.

According to stories that my grandmother, who was over 100 years old, had told me, the Bubu was initially used in witchcraft ceremonies, but that quickly changed.

In recent decades, it has become the most popular type of music in Sierra Leone. It is played by a group of several strong young men with high stamina using self-made instruments. They were known for blowing on different lengths of bamboo cane channels and carburettor pipes, hitting the monstrous bass drum and timber boxes, and shaking the shakers and bells all to create a unique sound. All the members of this band were popular among the ladies.

The most popular man among them was whoever carried the big, heavy box around his waist. This box was sometimes made from timber designed to produce bass. When these different sounds are mixed accurately together with the hysterical handclaps, the beats may seem to be moving too fast. Yet, it somehow still had room for loud vocal trills that spread highlife and created ecstatic energy far and wide. This music was so vibrant and infectious that it created a popular notion in the Temne tribe: that regardless of how sick someone is, if the Bubu is played and a person does not move any part of their body, then that person would die. For the well and able, the Bubu session could sometimes last the whole night; the band and the people would travel via foot from town to town, covering over ten miles.

The crowing began in the morning. It was time for the messenger to start his journey with the cow back to my father's village, Madina. The messenger arrived in Madina late in the evening with the gift; the villagers welcomed him with loud cheers.

My mother explained to me how she had felt in the first weeks after she had arrived in Madina. Since she knew no one—not even the man she had married— she cried for weeks. The sense of loss of family and friends had almost been too much for her. Sendoku, her own village, was everything to her, and her marriage to my father brought all but happiness to her life. She had married him merely out of a sense of duty, and she felt the sheer helplessness of a naïve, young girl.

Madina was known for the seven famous red houses at the south entrance of the town. These houses were the only painted houses in that region. My father and his brothers owned these first seven houses at the entrance to Madina. Why red? Well, you see, red symbolises dominance. The red houses struck fear into the other tribe members. My father was from the Temne tribe, like my mother. My uncles had the largest farms. Of them, the youngest brother, Saliu, had a garden surrounding the entire village with a variety of mangoes, oranges, pineapples, and guava, to name a few.

Madina was designed like a crocodile with one right leg. The elders in the town that controlled the farming, vegetation and money were the crocodile's head, located in the south. The less fortunate, poor villagers were situated in the corner of the village, which was the leg of the crocodile located in the east part of the town. The body and the crocodile tail of Madina were the lawmakers.

My father was not in any of these categories. He was a diamond digger.

Sierra Leone is known for its precious rocks; a quarter of the country has diamonds. The Kono district is the central spot for mining. 20 days after my parents got married, my father decided they would travel to Freetown, the capital city of Sierra Leone.

They made this journey using the *Poda Poda*, which is a van commonly used by those travelling to and from the capital. The van is designed to fit about eight passengers in the back and two in the front.

There is a saying in Sierra Leone that in this van, you are 'choked like sardines' because of the almost suffocating amount of people in one single van. Some drivers would have up to 16 passengers in the back and four in the front, and to save money, some people would choose to sit on the laps of others. There was no public transport in Sierra Leone. It was either taxi or the Poda Poda.

As congested as this form of transportation is, it always provides an interesting travelling experience. There are people from different parts of the country in it, including foreigners. It provides an environment to share stories, tell jokes, and even test vocals whenever the driver decides to play some cultural or popular music. As cramped as the space is, everyone is 'as happy as Larry'.

Another unique feature of the Poda Poda is that it allows people to advertise their ideologies. On the outside, at the front of every Poda Poda, the owners would write in big, bold, and colourful writing things like 'Respect your neighbour', 'Jesus is Lord', 'Allah is one', 'Fear judgment day' and many more.

I would guess that in Sierra Leone, when I was a child, the population was made up of approximately 70% Muslims, 20% Christians, and a small fraction of people that don't identify with any religious belief. Despite Islam and Christianity being so distinctively different, Sierra Leoneans agree we are all one, and we all have one God. This norm created the space for everyone to freely express their religious faith and make Mama Salon (the nickname for Sierra Leone) the spiritually tolerant place it is.

Eastern Police, a street in the heart of Freetown, Sierra Leone's capital city and one of the popular stops for every Poda Poda driver. People travelling from the city to the village would usually stop in every big town to buy bread. If a person was going to the village, one of the expectations was for them to give loaves as a gift. My parents were travelling from the village to the city, so they purchased oranges, groundnuts, and fresh cow's milk to take as a gift. The distance from my town to the city was approximately an eight-hour drive.

It was during one of these stops that my father first told my mother that he had another wife. Mother wasn't surprised; she told me so herself years later. In Sierra Leone, it had become the norm and it was generally expected that men marry multiple wives.

When my parents arrived at Eastern Police, my father took my mother to stay with one of his friends for a few hours. He went to his two-bedroom apartment, which he was renting with his first wife, who I will call Elder Mama. He was going to tell her about my mother.

When my father reached Elder Mama's place and told her about my mother, she broke down into tears. She was disappointed and kept blaming herself.

"Have I not been a good wife?" she asked as the sobs racked her body. "Is this a punishment?"

Of course, it wasn't, but there wasn't anything my father could say to comfort her. It was already very late, around 10 pm, so my father had to go and fetch my mother, who was still at his friend's house.

When my father arrived home for the second time, he was with my mother. It was Elder Mama's first son who opened the door.

"This is my son," he said, and gestured towards the first son, Hass. Nowadays, Hass is the head of our polygamous family. My mother was young and vibrant, and they would later build a strong connection. Hass would spend more time with my mother than his own. Hass is known for his temper, and we all feared him growing up. Whenever he was upset with one of our siblings, he would challenge them to a fight. Academically, he is the smartest in the family and would always get praise from our father. Our father constantly compared his results to that of our other siblings, especially my mother's second child, Abbigail. This was the beginning of the tension and rivalry in our polygamous family.

"This is the elder wife, Sento," my father said, introducing his first wife to my mother.

With that, the two women were officially introduced to each other. Just like that. Straight to the point without mincing words.

Both women burst into tears. Elder Mama was in her second trimester expecting her second child who turned out to be her first daughter. She was in no way prepared for her husband to return with a new wife. He was supposed to have merely travelled to the village. My father had given her no warning.

It was hard for my mother, too. She was struggling to adjust to married life since she had been given away so young and without her consent. Now, not only was she going to be a second wife, but the elder wife already had a son and was expecting another child. As both women stared at each other, the feeling of complete powerlessness, inconsideration, and awkwardness crept in.

You wouldn't exactly expect to open your door at 10 pm to your husband with another wife, would you?

Elder Mama walked back into her room, shoulders dropped, and sniffing back hot tears. Father crept across the living room into the other room while my mother tiptoed carefully behind him.

Hass, Elder Mama's first child, watched the drama quietly unfold. As a child, it was confusing enough to be introduced to a new parent at 10 pm one night. Worse still, he had to give up his room for my mother and was given a lappa to use as both a sheet and a blanket. The living room was his new sleeping space.

Whew! Poor boy. He must have wished everything was just one terrible dream and that he would wake up the next morning to just him, his mother, and father, as they had always been. Too bad my mother was there to stay.

According to my mother, for the first few months, father wouldn't enter her room or be intimate with her because he was trying to make it up to Elder Mama.

My mother was expected to do all the house chores: cleaning, cooking, fetching water, and brooking (washing) everyone's clothes.

For brooking in Sierra Leone, people use the washing board. The washing board is made from wood and has a solid, ridged surface. The clothes are soaked in big washtubs with soap for 5-30 minutes, then rubbed against the washing board's ridged surface to force all the dirt out of the clothes. It was built to withstand strength and flexibility, which made it suitable for everyone from children to adults, regardless of the garment.

This old-fashioned equipment saved energy and was water efficient. It was the perfect equipment for a household. My parents' home, on the other hand, was far from perfect. It was in this kind of environment that my mother began her new duties as the second wife. Naïve and young, without any guidance, she would learn through experience what it really meant to become a wife and a mother. In the events to come, she would learn from her mistakes and grow in the process. To be young and free-spirited was a luxury she would never be afford.

CHAPTER 2

The Triangle of Two Wives

It had been three months since Elder Mama and my mother started living together in the same household. There was my father, two wives, and children squeezed together, struggling to survive on the already-meagre income he could provide. Father was the sole provider and breadwinner of our polygamous family. Trying to see things in a positive way, during hard times like this, was like finding a needle in the ocean.

In such a condition, tension was unavoidable as my mother told me, and as I also learnt later. You couldn't escape it. There was always fear, stress, uncertainty, and helplessness floating in the air. Both wives had their fair share of it, each somehow managing to steer clear of the other's boundaries. But not for long, for in a polygamous house, even if you sat still and did nothing, trouble would still find its way to you. It did not take too long to find my mother.

As the second wife, my mother was the new bride. The one who was yet to conceive or bear a child. The one whose role was now primarily taking care of household chores and cooking. My mother would sometimes need Hass' assistance to carry out the chores, but he seemed to have abandoned all his tasks to her.

You're the new wife, the woman who's come to make mother cry, he may have thought I imagined. There would be enough reason in his head to want to punish her by refusing to participate in any of the household chores again.

And for my mother, she was in unfamiliar territory.

She was a stranger who had invaded another woman's space. She had to tread cautiously when trying to discipline Hass.

This was another woman's son. One wrong move could very well be misinterpreted. Most times, my mother would rather ignore the problem than complain to Elder Mama about Hass' attitude. The few times she did complain, the weird feeling and fear she received quickly discouraged her from further attempts.

Something as simple as asking, 'Why didn't you do the dishes?' could be the starting point of a big conflict, and that was something my mother desperately tried to avoid.

Then, the tension between the two wives had another fuel added. This time, it was unavoidable. Both women were stuck.

You see, Elder Mama was already pregnant with her second child, Sata, when my mother arrived. And as expected of her, my mother immediately relieved Elder Mama of her cooking tasks.

Cooking in itself was not a big deal, but cooking for a pregnant woman was a different thing altogether. In addition to her mood swings, Elder Mama's pregnancy made her crave different foods. Sometimes, she would not like the taste of my mother's food or the way it was prepared.

In Sierra Leone, *plasas* (sauce) was a very common household meal, and my mother liked to make it. It was made with greens like cassava leaves, potato leaves, or spinach mixed with meat to create stew plasas. The cassava is a shrubby, tropical plant in Sierra Leone. Its leaves and roots are edible.

To make this delicacy, the cassava leaves are washed and pounded using mortar and pestle (*matta odo*, in my native dialect). It is then gently cooked with salt, chili, white Maggie (seasoning cubes) and fresh palm oil infused with dry, smoked, delicious Bonga (fish) to give your lips a unique, satisfying tingle. Onions were not added unless you were among the privileged.

The sumptuous plasas is served with rice, which is the staple food in Sierra Leone. It is quite significant because it served as an incentive and fuelled the hardworking man. Among the locals, it was well established that this meal tasted better the following day than it did the day it was cooked.

Often, a family could decide to eat a little bit during dinner and save the rest for breakfast to eat as cold *res* (rice). Cold res was the breakfast that made lunch unnecessary. There was also the mouth-watering *krawo*, capable of turning a silly child good for a week if promised a taste. In this case, the rice had to be mixed with the cassava leaves and allowed to sit on the pot. Next, heat would be applied until a sizzling sound could be heard. That was when you'd get the crispy, perfect krawo.

This, along with any meat in the sauce, was reserved for the elders. As a kid, when asked if you had eaten breakfast, the only time a 'yes' would be uttered was if the breakfast was rice or some other products made from cassava. Imagine having eggs or fruits for breakfast and being asked, 'Have you eaten?' You'd think they'd count, wouldn't you?

However, a very loud 'no' would be the response,

for such light meals did not count. It was either rice with cassava or potato leaves, *binch* (beans), or spinach—nothing else was considered filling enough. Whatever you ate for breakfast had to fill you up until dinner. Lunch was not in the dictionary. It might sound wrong to have something so heavy for breakfast, but it surely did serve its purpose. We were able to use the limited food resources available. There is a fine line between eating just enough to keep you at best function throughout the day and being unpleasantly full. Anyways, this is no recipe story.

Now, back to Elder Mama's cravings. Even if she did not like the taste of the food or suddenly changed her mind about the meal being prepared, it was considered very rude to refuse. She had to simply make do with what was prepared no matter how upset she was. It was even worse if she decided to prepare her own food. It was in this environment that my mother was expected to cook. The custom and culture of our people prohibited Elder Mama from saying anything negative about the food. This way of cooking was taught and passed down from generation to generation. Any show of objection was seen as an insult to the family of the person whose food you rejected.

As if the triangle of the two wives couldn't get any more complicated, there was the next most serious issue in the household. The issue of sexual relationships. It was commonly referred to as 'the nights' by the adults. This meant the number of times the husband would sleep in each woman's room. You might be wondering how that would work for a man with multiple wives, but they really did find a way to make it work. Marrying multiple women was common for those who occupied positions of power, usually the chiefs. Some of them married up to four wives. For them, they had to adjust things to match the household and the number of wives involved.

For my parents, it was the three nights each. Three consecutive days with each woman. My father would head over to either Elder Mama's room or my mother's room depending on whose three days it was. My parents did not have any specific dates for when the three days began, as I later learned. They simply decided on it.

Soon, it was time for Elder Mama to give birth—or *born time*, as my people locally called it. Her water had broken, and she had been carried to the older women in the complex. These women were highly respected for their experience and skill when it came to matters of childbirth.

Ya Yainkain was the most senior of them all. She had given birth to nine children and was in charge of the other women who handled childbirth. While the women hustled about trying to put things in place in preparation for the delivery of Elder Mama's baby, my mother kept busy, preparing different meals in the kitchen. Unknown to her, she was just about to hear something that would forever change her life.

You see, around this time, my mother had begun to experience some symptoms of morning sickness, including vomiting. After preparing the meals and taking them to the Elder Mama, who had just given birth to her second child, Sata, my mother decided to approach one of the older women. She explained her symptoms while the woman examined her. She gave her the good news.

"You are with a child!" the older woman exclaimed before turning to the others in the room to spread the word.

It was a case of being both ecstatic and anxious. She was happy to share this news with my father, but she was also anxious. It was her first time, and she was worried about how this would affect the family and her relationship with Elder Mama.

She was right to be concerned. Arguments began over who my father should spend more time with. No matter what he did, he was accused of neglecting one wife and being biased towards the other. Well, he never could please two women equally. Or could he?

While the squabbles and arguments continued, there was a more pressing need to attend to the two women struggling for affections. At this stage, my father had not been to Kono to dig diamonds for a while, which was his primary occupation at the time. With no other job qualifications, he had to go out all day to look for odd jobs so he could find chop money (feeding money) for his growing family. At times, he would visit our relatives around the city for help in his search for jobs. In Sierra Leone, it was expected that when a family member visited, you had to give them their transport back home, and a little bit more, to return to their family. My father would visit one or two relatives during the week and then walk home to save the transport money so he could use it to provide for the family.

You might think this was easy, but some of my father's relatives lived very far away. Sometimes, he had to walk for five hours to get back home to save the transport money for feeding. Things were really tough, and father was barely managing to provide even the barest minimum for the family.

Soon, Elder Mama's daughter, Sata, was almost one year old, and my mother had given birth to a baby girl, Abbigail. She was the bubbly sister who always had a smile on her face. She was always caring, loving, and affectionate.

She had a round face with big eyes and thick eyebrows. A nature stamp (birthmark) on the left side of her lips made her infectious smile even more contagious—she looked just like our mother. Abbigail ended up being the one sibling that my father placed the entire Bangura family's fate on. She had to carry the entire family on her shoulders as early as her twenties. This is what it meant to be one of the eldest children.

To this day, she is an overachiever who constantly pursues her next conquest. Abbigail is the sibling I share many attributes with, like a hunger for success. We have an enemy-like relationship.

Four weeks later, there was a day that was far from a good one for my father. It was around 8 pm and the rain was pouring heavily with bouts of thunder and lightning flashing across the pitch-black sky. Father arrived home drenched, soaked from head to toe. That night, he called the entire family together, three young children and two wives, and he began lamenting about the current ordeal the family faced. With no job or business, it was a big struggle to pay rent and feed everyone, much less afford other necessities.

"Things are hard for me right now," Father began in a hushed whisper. "I need you people to go back to the village." His eyebrows creased with worry and his now aging shoulders slumped in defeat. Elder Mama was not having it. She cringed immediately at the words 'village' and 'go' uttered in the same sentence.

"I'm not used to doing farm work," she immediately chimed in.

Apparently, returning to the village would mean having to engage in farm work. In the village, you had to grow crops, clear bushes, and use manpower or physical labour to raise something productive from the farm. For Elder Mama, this was not an option. So, she decided to stay with a family member in Freetown along with her two children.

My mother had to quietly travel back to her family in Sendoku. Father, on his part, travelled to the diamond-rich Kono district to mine. Mining diamonds was very common for my people in Sierra Leone. It was like playing the lottery. The only difference was that the land was rich in diamonds, so much so that the precious, sparkling gem was sometimes visible on the ground after a hefty downpour of rain. People mined in small and large groups scattered all over the Kono

Rivers.

According to Father, mining was a physically demanding job where people had to use shovels and other digging equipment, depending on their status, to find diamonds. You could sometimes spend 12 hours bending over in the river, washing mud, and shaking sieves, searching for sparkling gems. Nothing was guaranteed. You could do this all day, all week, and even all month, without finding even one gem.

Now that I think of it, my father might have been poor earlier on, but he was a good man. He did not take what wasn't his and had strong moral values. It was this honesty that made his group decide to make him the leader. He was responsible for sourcing equipment, food, and other things needed to keep the mining group working together.

Father quickly grew connections and networks in the area. Sometimes, someone he knew would find *nark* (a diamond), sell it, and share the profit with close friends. He formed a ten-man group in the mining district and rented a two-bedroom apartment. That was when he sent a friend to bring Elder Mama and the two kids to Kono.

Two months after their return to Kono, a member from Father's mining group was washing the mud off stones and saw a small gem sparkling like nothing he had seen before. He lifted the sieve and called to my father, causing their small group of miners to gather around in excitement. Father took the gem and inspected it. The entire team shouted in pure happiness. Excited chatter broke out among the men. Everyone came together for a group hug. This was a huge win for the group.

In the midst of all this, my mother had became pregnant with her first son before she left. A few months later, while she was asleep, she woke up to blood all over the bed. She was rushed to an elderly woman in the area during the night, and it was confirmed that she'd had a miscarriage—the baby had died.

My mother went through a hard time coming to terms with this loss. It was the first time this had happened to her. My father spent extra time with her, and Elder Mama took over some of the household chores. The situation at home had greatly improved ever since the three-carat diamond was found. My father could purchase gifts like a six-yard lappa to surprise each of our mothers.

My mother proved to be very efficient during this period. As a coping mechanism, my mother decided to stay busy. She assisted my father by providing meals and other resources for the workers since she had lost her baby. But it wasn't for long. After one rainy and one dry season passed, my mother began to experience nausea, light-headedness, and sore breasts. She made a visit again to the same elderly woman who had confirmed her miscarriage earlier.

This time, there was good news. She was pregnant again. It had been nine months since the miscarriage. My mother had only Abbigail and the miscarriage. Elder Mama had a son, a daughter, and twins (Cynthia and Alus), which gave her four children. In total, my father had six children.

Now, you would think my father would no longer desire any more children since his household was becoming large, but that was far from the case. If anything, things were about to become more interesting.

My mother's daughter, Salamatu, child number three, the Mother Theresa of the Bangura family, was born.

Picture this ... Our family is huge. One father, two wives, and 24 children. There is bound to be conflict, mischief, and disagreements along the way. Even though the wives functioned as a family unit, each wife wanted their children to succeed and thus groomed an unspeakable but affirmed notion of competitiveness among the children. The positive impact of this resulted in each child striving to overachieve and exceed their limits, especially in school, to win the favour of our father and the pride of their mother. On a negative note, this bred contempt and jealousy among the children. To this day, there is a great divide among the 24 children. Each sect sticks to their own unit.

My sister, Salamatu, is called the Mother Theresa of the family because of her resilience in solving issues within both sects and due to her soft, kind-hearted nature. She is the only sibling that is in contact and has good standing with each member of the family. Not once in my entire life have I heard anyone, family or not, utter a word of displeasure against this sister. For years, Salamatu was the mediator between both sects of the family. She was the person that every sibling went to for advice or to settle family matters. Everyone knew she was impartial and always spoke the truth. For that and more, she remains the most loved among all the siblings.

At a very young age, she became seriously ill and had to be rushed to the hospital. She was about two years old. She was given drips, drugs, and injections. In Sierra Leone, regardless of whatever medical condition you presented when attending a hospital, the first and maybe the only thing the doctors gave, would be a drip or an injection. It gradually became the norm for my people. To this day whether someone is seriously sick or not, if the doctor does not hang a drip on them or fails to give them an injection, they criticise the doctor and won't take such treatments seriously even if they eventually recover from the illness. You would even hear statements like, 'I went to the hospital today. They charged me so much money, yet the doctor only gave me Panadol or drugs. No drip! No injection! I must have been ripped off!'

But for Salamatu, despite receiving several drips and injections, her condition did not improve. She had been showing symptoms like a constant stomachache, loss of appetite, and weight loss. Her lack of responsiveness to the treatments at the hospital greatly worried my parents, so they decided to try another alternative. The alternative was for my mother to take her to Sendoku to try the native herbal route, also called the *contree way* by my people. My parents upheld strong cultural and religious beliefs, so they often trusted and relied more on natural remedies through native doctors and herbalists than English doctors. Besides this, another major factor in their choice to opt for traditional medicine was its affordability. The native remedies, compared to the English medications, were less expensive and even more easily accessible. It was like killing two birds with one stone—a no-brainer. My mother travelled the next day by Poda Poda to take her second daughter to Sendoku while being in her third trimester with another child.

As days turned into weeks and weeks into months, my sister did not get any better. My mother gave birth to Sheik, child number four. Exhausted and out of resources to continue further treatments, my mother decided to return to Kono. She left Sheik behind.

Sheik is the gangster-turned-religious leader. He was the most honest sibling amongst us all. Sheik was the most obedient and loving to our parents. He never said no to our mother. He took over the role of our father, especially after he had passed. Sheik inherited our father's philosophy of bearing many children.

Today, he is a well-respected and celebrated member of our community. Sheik is the one who is always there for me in any situation. Our relationship continues to grow, but with some conflicts as his strong religious philosophy clashes with my modern, Western approach to things.

Anyways, my mother and Salamatu headed back to Kono. For the first time in years, both wives were in Kono together, each occupying a separate room. One can only imagine how they lived together, knowing that there were more children than before and even more on the way—my mother had returned to find out that Elder Mama was pregnant with the second sets of twins. As for the children, they all slept together in the *pala* (living room).

Living together with two mothers allowed the children to learn from both of them. As time passed, they grew accustomed to taking directions and orders from either mum. Subsequently, the friction and tension between both women regarding who was permitted to discipline a child lessened. When a child misbehaved, it was up to either Father, my mother, or Elder Mama to discipline them, depending on who received the complaint.

The popular disciplinary method for kids back then was to get them to cross their arms, hold the opposite ear in each hand, and squat a hundred times. It was popular because of its effectiveness when executed. It would weaken their muscles to the point where they would regret to their core whatever wrong they did.

Another popular one was usually aided by elder siblings, especially brothers. They would hold you by the arms and legs, stretch you on the floor, and the parent would take over from there. Using a belt or small bamboo stick as a whip, they would whoop the child on their backside a dozen or two dozen times, depending on the severity of the offence. I think our parents must have had superhuman strength then, because they could whip all ten children a dozen strokes each and not get tired.

Nearly all the methods of discipline involved the use of physical force. Every child went through it. It didn't matter how good you were; you could never be perfect, so you would have to taste the bitter whip at least once, and more if you were a naughty or stubborn child. The one method that didn't require physical force was the hunger method. This meant that the offending child would not be allowed to have dinner as a form of discipline. I think us kids preferred physical punishment over being starved. This was the greatest form of torture. Sitting at home in the corner of the pala and smelling the delicious fried onions and mouth-watering, freshly cooked cassava leaves while your stomach hosted a royal rumble match, knowing full well it would be deprived of the delicacies, was the worst. As a result, it was not unusual to see a child bawling their eyes out, pleading for his punishment to be changed to whipping. Yes, that was the power of good food.

Elder Mama had given birth to the twins—children five and six, Binty and Tereza. One of the benefits of our large family was the fact that there was never a dull moment. The children learned to play together, live together, and fight together. We often clashed in opinions. This was the basis for our unity, for some periods at least. After each fight, we had to make up, and this strengthened the bond we shared as siblings. Some kids grew a strong bond with the other parent and even preferred one parent's cooking style over the other.

As our family tree expanded, our resources dwindled. With more mouths to feed, my father had even more expenses, and the mining business was experiencing a dry season. Although Kono blossomed with diamonds, there were hundreds of miners that each sought the special gem my father wanted, too. My father and his group mined in an area where there were rumours of diamonds existing underneath the earth. My family was in a dark place, and they chose to look forward to the sunrise. The whole group was optimistic and hopeful that they would find the gem they sought. Jokes even began to fly around that my mother would give birth to the baby that would bring luck to the group, since she was pregnant at that time.

Six months passed, and the area had almost been completely excavated with few portions remaining. The group began to lose hope. Perhaps the stories were false and there were no diamonds in the area. All their hard work and resources had been put into this project and each member of the group desperately needed money for their family's survival.

Other groups moved out of the area to scout for greener pastures. Father was greatly worried. If a miracle did not happen, his small group of miners, who had become like family to him, would have to disband and go their separate ways.

Would a miracle happen? Father had no idea. All he knew was that the family needed one, and if it were not forthcoming, the impact would severely cripple the entire household. In the meantime, they could only work, pray, and wait.

CHAPTER 3

A Miracle is Born

As my mother's delivery time drew closer, my father's apprehension increased. We were going to have a new addition to the family and the sky still seemed bleak. What was he going to do? Where would the family go from there? Numerous thoughts plagued him as he and his group of miners tirelessly dug the earth. They were bare backed with the sun burning their dark, etched skin; sweat dripped to the ground and their hands were covered with mud, yet they were unwilling to give up. On the days when the sun was too hot, they would drip sweat from the crown of their heads to the soles of their feet, yet the constant sound of their equipment digging through the earth never stopped. Father never missed a day with the group, until one particular day came along.

My mother woke up having contractions and Father had stayed home to help her. That day marked the last day of mining that site. Everyone had been optimistic enough, yet it was time to be realistic. No miracle was coming. They would finish work on the site as planned and plan their next move. Two hours into labour, my mother gave birth to a blue-eyed, wavy-haired girl with glowing, beautiful, black skin— child number five for my mother. As if on cue, at that same time, Father's mining group arrived home, their shovels were over their heads and their hands were muddy, yet their faces beamed with smiles and excitement. They were hugging each other and singing their favourite Bubu site song, which when translated, meant: 'Look! this is how we are going to go about it this year, this is how, this is how, this is how, and then the other way!'

They were so excited and rowdy, that each one was raising his voice against the other in pure delight. Soon, the kids joined in the merrymaking. The men grabbed Father, lifted him up, and danced around the pala. Their actions surprised Father, who was both anxious and confused. He even admitted that the group was laughing a little too hard, singing a bit too enthusiastically, and dancing a bit too intensely for his daughter's birth.

Everything made sense when one of the boys yelled out in excitement. "We're naming her Diamond! She brought us luck, indeed!"

The group had found what they were looking for: diamond. This time it much bigger than the first one. They had been toiling for months and finding this diamond was a miracle. Father heaved a deep sigh of relief: indeed, a miracle had been born, and the child was named Diamond.

You would think the group would eagerly rush back to the site to continue digging in the hope of finding more gems, wouldn't you? But for a week, the bunch did not set foot on the site—or any other site, for that matter. They rewarded themselves with a vacation and spent their days eating and playing drafts (checkers), which was popular and addictive. It was the equivalent of a modern-day video game. The men would sometimes play for 12 hours nonstop, except when it was time to eat or use the bathroom. Those not playing sip on their *poyo*, a local palm tree wine drink mainly made in the villages in Sierra Leone. This adult milky-white, frothy beverage contained about 1% alcohol. As the saying goes, it was made 'from God to man'. It was meant to be drunk straight from the tree and not mixed with anything; it was to be enjoyed as a naturally pure, refreshing, mildly alcoholic drink.

Before baby Diamond, none of the other children had been given a naming ceremony or a *pull na dou,* as we called it locally. In Sierra Leone, especially in the Temne Muslim tribe, the tradition when you had a son was to slaughter two sheep, and one sheep for a daughter. Diamond's coming brought immense luck to the family. Therefore, a naming ceremony was arranged for her. Most gatherings in Africa tends to be boisterous and filled with people who are extremely energetic, loud, or simply gluttonous. However, if you dropped a pin during the pull na dou, you would hear it. That was how solemn this occasion was, and everyone was respectful of the tradition and listened attentively. Once the ceremony was concluded, everyone dispersed slowly with their takeaway containers. Like the name implied, takeaway meant something to take away or take back. When you hear the word takeaway, ordering at a local fast-food restaurant might be the first thing on your mind. Well, in Sierra Leone, things worked differently. Whenever there was a celebration, the hosts would have to cater for double the amount of people they expected to come. Why? Because of takeaway.

Everyone expected to eat and still have a container of food prepared for them to take back to their family. This unwritten rule was so important that people would criticise you if you just catered for them to eat for the occasion. With Diamond's celebration, takeaway was prepared and there was more than enough for everyone to eat.

Baby Diamond was a beautiful child. Her blue eyes charmed everyone, and she was passed from one person to another for good luck. This was the child who brought a miracle, and everyone wanted a touch of her.

The very next day, everyone gathered in the living room to make a very important decision that would change our lives. All the children sat on the dusty, concrete floor with their legs crossed, facing the main speaker, our father, who sat in the centre of the room on the three-seater, sky-blue sofa. Each wife took a seat beside him. Father wanted to listen to suggestions and opinions from everybody.

"What are we going to do with my share of the diamond money?" he asked.

"A house! A house! Yes, let's buy a house," everyone agreed.

After three tedious months of searching, the house buying process was finally completed. They chose a house on Kissy Road, one of the prime locations in the city of Freetown. A blue, six-bedroom, double-story house was the perfect solution for the mighty family of 11 children.

My sister, Salamatu, had not had an easy life. Her

life has been fraught with danger and hardship since she was young. Father's younger brother, Thaimu Bangura, and his wife, Jasmine, requested that Salamatu go live with them when she was a teenager. They vowed to take care of her. Thaimu is the leader of the political People Democratic Party (PDP). He is a very famous and influential person in Sierra Leone. During his final year of studying politics in England, he met, fell in love with, and married Jasmine. They had been married for a few years at that time.

Salamatu transferred to Barbadore to live with Thaimu and Jasmine in their 12-bedroom house that was surrounded by a two-meter-high fence. Approximately 3,000sqm of land was covered in all types of fruits, like *pawpaws* (papayas), oranges, bananas, mangoes, lemons, and guavas, all aesthetically planted across the compound. To be taken in to live in a place like this is like playing the lottery. Salamatu quickly recovered from her ongoing stomach pains and loss of appetite. She was trusted to start looking after some arrangements in the house.

Upon Father's return to Kono, new trouble was brewing. The diamonds had become scarce. New equipment was needed, the mining group had to be fed, and the money he had left was dwindling fast. As if those concerns weren't enough, Elder Mama was pregnant again with child number seven, Haji, and my mother was pregnant with child number six. So, my father found himself with two pregnant women, one in Kono and the other in Freetown, with almost no money.

The money from the sale of the last diamond had been invested in the house and used towards other expenses. There were flocks of children to feed in addition to his wives and himself. How long could whatever money he had last anyway?

As for the group, well, they too had used up their own shares of the money. They hoped they would be blessed with another diamond. Imagine!

This time, luck was far from them. The equipment they used was getting worn out and needed to be replaced. The once jolly group became disgruntled and began to complain. Some even threatened to leave the group and return to farming. The news about the current situation in Kono reached my mother, who was in Freetown. She boarded the next Poda Poda with Diamond and went back to Kono. She had an excellent relationship with the group and decided to address matters. Since she arrived late at night, she headed to the site early the next morning and gathered the group members together.

"Remember where you came from and how all of you are now family. This is temporary, and we will get through this rough patch together." Her wise words inspired them to stay and continue to work together.

Meanwhile, Elder Mama had given birth to Haji, the lover boy of the family. He was the smooth talker that now has numerous kids with multiple women. He also observed our father's ideology of having a vast family. Due to his stubbornness and womanising ways, he constantly clashed with the first son and transgressed into vicious enmity with Hass as the years went by.

The group mined for months, but there were no signs of the situation improving. Father decided to travel back to Freetown with Elder Mama and Haji to try to hustle around for money to continue funding the mining project. At the time, my mother was due to give birth in a few weeks.

Life was not prepared to cooperate with my father. Rejection after rejection followed and Father was not able to borrow enough money. The situation was so terrible that there was literally nothing to eat for days—even weeks. With a young child still suckling and another wife due to give birth, Father weighed his options carefully and chose the last resort. The new house in Freetown would have to go. What use was a beautiful house when the household was starving?

Therefore, he decided to sell the house and rented two bedrooms on Gory Street. I guess it was back to square one at this point. But one could never be too sure. My mother had just given birth to child number six, who died a few hours after birth.

Earlier, I compared diamond digging to playing the lottery. And the most common trait of lottery players is that they are always hopeful. Even if they lose one round, they will attempt to play again with more hope of winning each time. Father was that way too with diamond digging. He was hopeful that his diamond mining would make him rich the next day, or the day after, and so on.

At this stage, another family member from my father's side decided she wanted to help us. She offered to adopt Sheik, Cynthia, and Haji. All three siblings were taken as *menpikin* (adopted) at Hill Station, Freetown. God bless her! This greatly lightened my father's load and lifted a few weights from his sunken shoulders.

The act of handing over your children for adoption went two ways. The child was either fortunate and was received into a home that was better and more caring, or the child was unlucky and was received into a home where they would be constantly abused and traumatised. Often, those children never grew out of the trauma and scars that followed such abuse.

This reminds me of January 2020, when my brother, Sheik, and I were expressing gratitude as we drove to lunch in Liverpool, Sydney, Australia. My brother suddenly began to reminisce about the past. He narrated the things he had to endure when he was a menpikin.

"I would wake up at five in the morning to fetch

water for Auntie's children so that they could take a shower before heading to school from Monday to Friday," he spat the words with contempt. I burst into laughter. "I had to make breakfast, lunch, and clean the entire house, but nothing was ever enough," he continued. "And as a menpikin, it didn't matter what happened. It was always your fault."

Sometimes, the parents of the menpikin knew about the struggles and abuse, but what could they do? Ask you to come back home and starve? Merely having someone take your child as a menpikin was a privilege and the highest form of help. Who would dare say anything?

Family members were often a huge support in times like this, but sometimes, it was not the case. You see, some family members would adopt these children to work for them and their children.

If you had the chance to ask my parents a question at this very point, you would probably ask, "If you could not afford to look after your child, why give birth to them in the first place?" After all, they were nobody's primary responsibility except the parents.

Six months had passed after my mother lost her sixth child, and she was already pregnant again with child number seven.

As I later learned from my parents, abortion was not an option available at that time. It was not just because of the cultural and religious expectations, but because you would not find someone to do it even if you wanted to. As for condoms, well, that was something of the new generation.

Now that these facts have been established, one can only imagine how hard it must have been for most families like mine. Sex was unavoidable. So, pregnancy was inevitable. People just continued to have sex and give birth to children until they were no longer able to. That was how it was. And having two wives meant the number of children doubled.

Above all, there was another major reason why people gave birth to several children. It was hoped that when they aged, their children could provide food, shelter, and medicine for them.

I'm not complaining that my parents had lots of children. After all, if I wasn't born, who would be telling you this juicy story? I guess I was God's plan since my parents were able to continue bearing children and stopped right after me.

Back to Kono, where the mining was continuing, the group had still not found any diamonds. The money from selling the house was still funding the project, but it was quickly running low as the months passed. It had been well over 5 months with no luck, and everyone was barely hanging on by a thin thread.

But like a true lottery player, Father had a feeling that things would get better. So, he continued to sell everything he had just to fund the mining project. My mother gave birth to child number seven, Baida. She was taken as menpikin as soon as she stopped breastfeeding. Baida is the mischievous sibling in the family. She was always rebellious and never conformed to society's (or our family's) expectations about gender roles. She was the sibling that loved to act like a bloke and would terrorise an entire community should anyone offend her. Baida was loving, but at the same time, she was critical and harsh.

During the civil war, Baida was captured and taken

prisoner. However, she used that to her advantage and fell in love with her captor. She even went as far as to have a child for him. She used to tell our family stories of her adventures.

Elder Mama was pregnant with child number eight, Sidu. By this time, the house was gone, and Father was selling some old equipment to keep the mining operation going. The mining group was also getting smaller as some members chose to return to farming.

The real eye opener came soon after that. Everyone in the group left. They could no longer continue. With no money and no workers, my family decided to sell the rest of the mining equipment at a substantial discount and head back to Freetown with all the kids.

Six Gorey Street in Freetown was a huge, old apartment with two bedrooms and a small living room. These apartments sometimes had up to ten family members occupying one unit. None of the apartments ever had a toilet or shower in them. There were five small rooms that each had a hole in the ground used as a toilet for all the tenants. They were built downstairs about six meters from the communal kitchen space. A maximum of five people could access the kitchen area to cook at the same time. People took turns cooking, and the tenants also took turns cleaning the toilets. On some days, when someone decided not to clean it on time, you would see white worms crawling on the walls and doors.

In my family's apartment, Elder Mama and my mother occupied one room each. The bed in their room had to be single to save space so the kids could store their two or three items of clothing. At night, the girls had to sleep in the living room while the boys slept on the veranda.

I do not know how long my parents stayed in Freetown. I learnt that my mother had two more children, child number eight, Abdul, and child number nine, Thaimu. Elder Mama had child number nine, Isabella, and child number ten, who died shortly after birth.

The little bit of cash Father brought with him was finished at this point, and the only option left was to sell the car.

This was not an easy decision for Father to make.

Besides being a source of pride to him, this was the only item of property he had left—the only thing he could call his own. Father agonized over it for days. This was rock bottom. How much worse could it get?

As we came to find out, it could get much worse.

At this point, you would think my parents wouldn't have more children. But soon, the number of children climbed to a total of 19, with just a few serving as menpikin. My mother was also weeks into a new pregnancy. There was nothing left to think about. Surely, the car had to go. With the landlord knocking on the door every morning for his overdue monthly rent and the kids struggling and barely able to eat, Father was not in the best circumstance to negotiate. Even though he had wanted to sell the car for a high bid, he was running out of time with each break of dawn. He had to accept the below-value offer he was given.

So, there they were: Father, Elder Mama, and my mother, in the living room, staring at the price of the Land Rover in valuable cash, contemplating the best ways to spend the money. Finally, they decided to pay the rent for the year and use the little that remained to buy food. The pressure eased for a short while, but Father was deeply saddened about selling the car.

Time flew by quickly during this period, especially with Father being idle. Eight months had passed, and he still hadn't been lucky enough to find a job. This time, there was nothing—absolutely nothing—left to sell. Late one rainy Saturday afternoon in July, my mother gave birth to child number ten. Most of the children had grown up, and some became old enough to work, but couldn't find a job. Father decided to call a meeting and address everyone.

"Things are hard right now for me. I am asking your mothers to go back to the village."

The room was as silent as a graveyard. No one uttered a word for several minutes until, finally, my mother responded to Father's desperate plea. "I will go back to the village."

Elder Mama was not on the same page as her co-wife. She told my father, "I'm not used to doing farming work, and I do not want to go to the village. I'm staying."

With that, an agreement was reached. It took my mother four months to prepare for her return to Madina. After four months and ten days, child number ten, Khalid, had a fever in the morning. Before nightfall, he died in my father's arms. A week later, my mother took all the children, besides those who had already been adopted by other family members and returned to the village. Only the first daughter, Abbigail, opted to remain.

"I'll stay in Freetown with a friend," she announced.

It was a long and emotional day for everyone when my mother and the children left. Mixed emotions and apprehension filled the air. Father tried to appeal to the family to forget the past decisions that had resulted in the family's current painful situation. While it was one thing to want to move on from the past, one cannot deny that the past can leave unforgettable scars that last a lifetime.

The family occupied the seventh red house in Madina. Early the following day after they arrived in the village, my mother implemented her plan. She paid a visit to the town headman (chief) to ask for land to farm. The land around the town had already been taken, and the only land available was at Bantamu, which was an hour's walk from the village. My mother accepted it gratefully. What was an hour walk to her if it meant she had food to feed her children?

In the following weeks, my mother arranged to buy rice and peanuts, and even prepared to clear the land so that planting could begin. My mother and the children walked an hour to the farm at 5 am each day. The blisters my mother got from digging up the ground made her hands feel like a washing board. She was a tough woman. If life handed her lemons, she was going to make fresh lemonade.

In Sierra Leone, whenever the rain came, it usually came down very heavily. Sometimes, these rainfalls would last for seven days and nights. The eighth child, Abdul, nicknamed the famous P-to-P, decided to imitate the other farmers by building a farmhouse for my mother.

His inexperience made things hard for him. Unknowingly, he built the farmhouse in the path of the water. When the rain poured heavily, the water created a path where it flowed like a river. The farmhouse was quickly swept away. For weeks after that, they worked under the rain, toiling and planting. Sometimes, when the rain was too heavy, they would stand under the palm trees.

Despite the lack of farming experience, sheer determination to help didn't allow P-to-P to give up. He was the entrepreneur of the family. Even though we were poor, he was always looking for small business opportunities to explore. Although he was not the best-looking guy compared to the other siblings, he was the most charismatic, and the ladies loved him. He always struggled with his health, but that didn't stop him from striving to elevate our poor situation.

Having learnt from his mistake, P-to-P decided to build another farmhouse. This time, he used an area on the other side of the farm and used sticks and palm tree branches. In the area, most of the palm trees were very tall. To find a short one, he had to walk for hours into the bush, hunting like a dog. For weeks, he kept hunting and searching, determined to end the heavy rain that drenched his poor mother and siblings each time they were out working on the farm. Some weeks, he would find one or two branches, but it was never enough. The only option that remained was to climb a tall palm tree. He had never climbed a palm tree before, let alone a tall one, but he was desperate to make things work. The rain and cold made his siblings sick. He tried to be a man for my mother since Father was not around.

He made a harness from rope and old clothes. Trial and error was another form of learning, wasn't it? Well, this one was far too risky to try but he did it anyways. Any mistake on his part meant he would fall from a palm tree that was over five meters tall. He would likely permanently damage his body or die. Thankfully, his harness was a successful experiment. It proved strong enough to hold him while he cut enough palm tree branches to complete the one-bedroom bachelor suite farmhouse. He used sticks for the walls and the palm tree branches for the roof.

Although everything seemed great on the surface, it wasn't quite what we had expected. The palm branches had to be stacked a certain way and the inexperienced P-to-P had done things the way he knew best. One afternoon, while the family was taking a break in the farmhouse, the sky quickly covered with dark clouds, and it soon began to pour. Within minutes, they noticed water dripping on their heads. The roof was leaking, and soon, the house was filled with water. That evening, everyone walked sombrely back home, soaked, shivering, and exhausted. The heavy rain was still pouring down, and they relied on the lightning to guide them home. Imagine walking under the rain in this condition and then getting struck by lightning. Though they did not get hit by lightning, they were all anxious that it would happen.

A few hours later after they reached home, the rain ceased. In the living room, the family discussed that though they appreciated the farmhouse, they intended to change the roof so it would keep out the rain.

The same evening, as they were getting ready for bed to rest up for another gruelling day at the farm, they saw the last Poda Poda of the evening pull over at the junction and let someone off. Everyone was waiting to see who it was. It was my father. He had come to check on my mother and the kids. He brought loaves of bread—a rare sight for the kids who could not remember the last time they had such a treat.

Diamond, P-to-P, and Thaimu all danced happily and stayed up late telling Father about the new experience on the farm. Thaimu was another entrepreneur of the family and preferred the city life way more than the village life. He wanted to move to the city.

According to my mother, she and my father had cried inside the room for hours once all the children had gone to bed.

"Things haven't improved for me, Marie," Father sobbed quietly. "I am in so much debt. Still no job. I do not even know if I'll be able to get one." He was inconsolable.

My mother held him close as the tears ran down his face. She knew very well how he was feeling. She felt the same way too: helpless and hopeless.

He continued his outpour to my mother. "People are chasing me every day to pay them the money that I owe. Oh, and Sento was pregnant a few months before you left. She has given birth to child number 11, RiRi."

This news weighed on my mother even more. More children meant more pressure, but what could she do?

Then, my mother had an idea.

Would it work?

She had no clue. But she had always been a woman of very strong faith. She was confident that if they tried something and it failed, it was better than not trying at all. She had to be strong and hopeful. If anything, she had children to look out for. In the hardest times, my mother chose to see things in a positive way.

With the mindset of a soldier, my mother decided to go into battle. Not a literal war, but one that meant battling doubts, mockery from the villagers, and worst of all, the absence of reasonable capital. My mother was never one to give up. She never did, and somehow this quality always served her for the best.

CHAPTER 4

The Strength of a Woman

With the farmhouse fixed and P-to-P now confident in climbing palm trees, my mother was ready to try out her idea. She would venture into palm oil production. My mother had never engaged in this type of business before. All her life, the only work she knew how to do well was centred around household chores, farm work or diamonds.

But my mother was an industrious woman, and she

was very brave. Once she set her mind to something, she achieved it against all odds. I think this is one of the many virtues my mother instilled in us as children: never give up, no matter what life throws at you.

In my mother's typical style, she, along with P-to-P, gathered fresh, ripe palm fruit bunches. In the early hours of the morning, P-to-P would first help with physically demanding tasks around the farm before heading to the bush to get palm fruits. Sometimes, he had to climb as many as 15 palm trees to get the amount of palm fruits needed.

Once he gathered a reasonable quantity, my mother cooked the palm fruit until it turned into a reddish pulp and the skin was removed. Next, she would pound it for hours to further soften it, remove the seeds, and finally cook the juicy skins again. It was this process that produced the most edible vegetable oil in Sierra Leone, and soon, my mother's hard work began to pay off.

Everyone in town and surrounding villages wanted to buy my mother's oil. As business picked up, she doubled her production. Within a few months, she had made enough money to sustain the household, and even saved some money, which she gave to Father to pay off his debts.

My mother was still basking in the glory of being the number one oil seller in Madina when she went into labour and gave birth to her 11th child, Musa. Just a few hours before, word arrived that Elder Mama had given birth to a baby, also a boy, her 12th child, Issa. He is the DJ in our family. His lifelong love and passion for music led him to become one of the most sought-after DJs in the state of New South Wales, Australia.

With such a big family, there is an unspoken rivalry. Despite the rivalry between the two families, Issa remained neutral in most instances, which allowed us to have a great sibling bond. We are close in age and have a similar mentality, and this has allowed us to build a strong friendship.

How many children does my already-huge family have now, you might wonder? Well, a little math wouldn't hurt.

Elder Mama now had 12 children in total: six sons and six daughters (including two sets of twins). My mother had 11 children in total: seven sons and four daughters. She lost child number two and child number six. Both were boys and both died at a very young age.

The grand total between both women was 23 children. That's right. 23 sons and daughters, more than the average number of players on a soccer team today. Like I so often say, maybe this was all God's plan. I mean, if my parents had stopped at child number ten or 15, where would that have left me?

As you know, I'm player No. 24. So, if you were thinking these people would have stopped giving birth by now, I'll have to disappoint you. Hang on as this game unfolds. You wouldn't be wishing I wasn't born, would you?

I say this with just a little trace of humour; maybe this was all God's plan. Who's to know if God and I made a deal and I had to be born despite all the odds. Maybe we had to keep the game going until player No. 24 arrived. Otherwise, who would be telling you this story? And who would have documented my family's experience during a very important time in Sierra

Leone's history? I choose to see the positives in this trauma and delusion.

For my mother and her children, there was no telling what would happen in the next few days or months to come. And even if by some magic it was possible to know, they would've had a hard time believing any of it. But life happens no matter what, and if there is anything I have learned, it is that life cares about nobody.

Another season had passed. Usually in our village, and Sierra Leone as a whole, people don't tend to like doing things when it rained. Farming activities and events were often cancelled when it rained. One day, it had rained the night before and P-to-P, who had become a little overconfident, still decided to take his usual trip into the forest.

Could it be that he had thought the rains from the night before would help saturate the palm fruits and make them even riper? Or had he simply grown impatient and decided taking a risk was better than waiting?

Well, I know not. But whatever it was that

prompted him to begin an early morning hike into the forest that fateful morning, he would soon question and regret his decision.

According to him, he climbed over ten palm trees that day, but on his way home, he had seen another one with juicy, ripe palm fruits on it. Even though it had started raining again, the overconfidence in him urged him to make the climb. So, he did. Throwing caution to the wind, he made his way nimbly onto the ragged exterior of the lone palm tree. He had only managed to cut the juicy palm bunch halfway through when his feet slipped on the wet tree skin. He fell right through his harness like lightning from the sky. His arms flailed desperately to hold on to anything he could. His back hit the hard, wet earth with a ghastly thud, and everything turned into darkness before his eyes. In times of adversity, you can choose to see things in a positive light, but for my brother, his eyes were closed.

No one saw him lying on the ground unconscious. Who with any good sense would be out in such a downpour? For hours, the rain poured fiercely, drenching his cold, unconscious body. When he finally regained consciousness, he dragged himself to the roadside, rolling and crawling in a bid to be seen.

He was quite lucky. He was finally spotted by the last farmer heading to the village. He ran to the village to ask for help.

You see, in the village—in fact, in Sierra Leone—whenever there was an accident or death, everyone would visit that house and begin to cry. Everyone sympathized with the person to whom the accident happened.

If you cared enough to listen to the people crying, you would hear them calling the names of all the people they had lost. It seemed as if they used other people's situations as an opportunity to remember their own deceased loved ones.

Think of it this way: Imagine you were ill at the hospital and a bunch of relatives and friends visited you. Now, picture them attempting to comfort you with stories of their own friends or acquaintances who had suffered similar illnesses and died. Not very comforting, is it?

That was exactly what played out in our house on

the day my brother, P-to-P, was brought home. He was barely able to breathe as he was carried over the shoulders of village youths.

The crowd had drawn closer to our house. Once the so-called sympathizers spotted my brother, they raised their voices even higher as if they'd been cued by a traffic light that turned green. Like a super sports car travelling from 0 to 100 mph, their cries could be heard from miles away.

Now that I think about it, I can only imagine how disheartened P-to-P must have felt hearing all that wailing. It probably sounded almost as if he were already dead.

For the rest of the night, my mother boiled water, dipped a clean towel in it, wrung it out, and placed it on his back. She wanted to keep him hot all through the night since he had spent hours bareback under the rain.

Early the next morning, people began to visit the house. Unlike the previous night, the cries were subdued. Maybe it was because he had survived the night, but things were much calmer and controlled as the women cried with my mother.

My mother paid several native doctors every day for nearly three months to try to heal him. The whole family went without sleep most nights as P-to-P cried, sweated, tossed, and turned, all while screaming in excruciating pain. It was a terrible ordeal for everyone, and often, the entire family would cry with him.

Every native doctor claimed to know how to heal him, and each one would request money, palm oil, goats, or sheep as payment before they would even begin treatment. Hope began to gradually fade away as the months passed. My mother had sold almost everything she had acquired to pay for treatment. Yet his situation did not seem to change. Despite this adversity, the sun still soared the next day. As I mentioned before, despite the circumstances, there is an opportunity to see things in a positive light. I am not saying it was good that P-to-P had an accident that nearly claimed his life, but if he hadn't had the accident, we wouldn't have met Samba. Samba, to me, is a superhero in this journey. And so, the universe unfolded as it should.

My mother was running out of options fast when news of a man named Samba from Macassa, 13 miles from Madina, was brought to her. According to the rumours and claims, he had healed many men who had been in a similar situation as P-to-P. Wasting no further time, Thaimu was sent to Macassa to call this man early the next morning. Since there was no money left, he had to walk to and from Macassa. Samba came to Madina three days later and assessed the situation.

"I need three days with him. Nobody should talk to us. Food should just be placed near the door, and only Marie can come in after every few hours to support the fourth son with toileting," he instructed. "I will charge you when this young man starts to walk again," he added confidently to everyone's surprise. And just like that, he began the treatments that were effective enough to heal P-to-P.

As he recovered rapidly, P-to-P needed a new business idea, since climbing would be out of the question for a long time. One day, he asked Diamond for a business idea.

She yelled almost immediately, "Bread! How about

we start making bread?"

Thaimu burst out laughing. "You just love your breads so much."

But P-to-P had gotten an idea from Diamond's suggestion and turned to Father eagerly. "A bakery. Father, do you know what I need to start a bakery? The world is oval and full of opportunities like a soccer field filled with soccer balls," he said, his face beaming with smiles. "From now on, call me Posts to Posts, or P-to-P, for short."

"P-to-P?" everyone asked curiously.

"Yes! Yes, P-to-P," he replied confidently.

And so, another dream was born.

Now, the only problem was that there was no flour. Therefore, Father promised to organise a few bags when he left for Freetown in a week's time. Upon hearing that my father was returning to the city soon, Thaimu asked if he could go, too. Surprisingly, Father agreed. Throughout the days that followed, the new bakery idea seemed to be what everyone was talking about.

On Saturday, after a breakfast of cassava leaves and cold rice, the final packing preparations commenced. My mother packed Thaimu's clothes and sent along some snacks like dried peanuts, oranges, papaya, and anything else she could get her hands on. The suitcases were cheap, matted, woven nylon zipped totes, commonly known as Ghana-must-go bags. Musa, Thaimu, and P-to-P carried them to the junction where Thaimu and Father were going to catch the Poda Poda.

As my mother later recounted, she had noticed that the luggage had seemed too high and heavy for the overcrowded vehicle and had pointed that out to the driver. The driver had been very defensive and dismissed her claims. He assured everyone that his apprentice knew what he was doing. As if to further buttress his defence, the apprentice had then used a very durable rope, the type used to tie troublesome cows to prevent them from entering people's farms, to tie the great loads onto the carriage above the Poda Poda.

Once this was done and goodbyes were said, the Poda Poda began its journey into Freetown. The kids ran excitedly after it until it left the village. Why children engaged in this intentional exercise would remain a mystery into adulthood. But one thing was for sure—your childhood was never complete if you did not run after a Poda Poda at least once in your life.

That evening, just as the first sign of darkness covered the sky, the family was having dinner when the last Poda Poda of the day arrived from Freetown. There was a certain sense of urgency and nervousness in the actions of the driver who hopped off at the junction. His words were fast, and he was almost sobbing.

"I have an urgent message for Marie SB. Does anyone know her house?" he asked those walking about on the road.

His actions and inquiries caught the attention of the town's chief, who asked one of the village's young men to lead the driver to where Marie SB lived.

As soon as my mother saw the driver's face covered in tears, she screamed very loudly and collapsed on the bare floor. The poor driver began to wail, too. In no more than a minute, the whole compound was flooded with villagers. Everyone wanted to know the cause of the commotion in Marie SB's house.

Some of the village women immediately responded to my mother's fainting spell by using cloth to fan her in an effort to resuscitate her. First aid, I presume, may have been the intent of this action. However, what sort of first aid involved a crowd of people attempting to rouse an unconscious person by simply fanning the individual with cloth?

Again, one can hardly blame anyone. People those days simply did what they could with the limited information they had. So, fan they did, until somehow, an hour later, my mother was conscious. Upon her recovery, the driver broke the news that she had feared. Something bad had indeed happened. There had been an accident, and Thaimu had died on the spot. As for Father, he had been seriously injured and was rushed to Connaught hospital.

My mother was five months pregnant at that time. Barely recovered from her fainting spell earlier, she sat on the floor, unable to talk or cry. She simply stared at empty space and was completely distraught.

Very early the next morning, without a single piece

of luggage, my mother boarded the first Poda Poda heading to Freetown. According to tradition, if someone died and their grave could be dug before the sun went down, then they had to be buried that day. My mother could not even see her son for the final time. As for Father, he had suffered only a few minor cuts and bruises. He was still in shock, more than anything else. His own son had died in front of his eyes, after all. My mother went to the hospital to check on my father and met with some of the elder children there.

The elder children walked my mother to the location of Thaimu's grave. Their destination was an hour away from the hospital. As soon as they approached the graveyard, my mother suddenly doubled her steps; she was almost walking and running at the same time. The very next thing they saw was my mother bending over to pull off her slippers before breaking into a quick sprint to the freshly dug grave.

The second she reached her target, she dropped to her knees. She placed both hands on top of the bare earth that encased the remains of her beloved son—

the sixth son. And then, with all the strength she could muster, she gave a heart-wrenching cry that only a mother's loss could evoke. Her lips quivered as the sobs shook her whole body. Her frame trembled and her screams and cries caused the birds in the surrounding trees to fly away. Knees pressed on the bare earth, she cried and cried some more. Her words were incoherent. Her nose was runny. Her eyes were bloodshot, and her face was stained with mud—which was the result of repeatedly burying her face in the freshly dug grave of her son. The other siblings knelt beside her with their palms lifted upwards. They muttered prayers of their own as she mourned.

An hour later, my mother was finally supported out of the graveyard and taken back to the hospital, where my father was. On seeing my mother's condition, Salamatu demanded that she stay with her for a bit at Barbadory, Freetown.

Salamatu had recovered from her ongoing stomach pains and loss of appetite. She was trusted to start looking after some arrangements in our uncle's house. She had become the house manager. This meant she was responsible for cooking, facilitating the cleaning of the compound, and attending to visitors' needs

As she progressed into adulthood, she met and married a young, educated, and ambitious man from the village, Mabaila. Our family and the entire village were proud when the village teller returned with the news that she was untouched (virgin), and her husband was her first. This made mother exceptionally happy. She had her first child while still living with my uncle, Thaimu Bangura.

Following Thaimu's burial, my mother's return to the village sparked new cries. It was as if everyone was waiting for her to return so they could resume their wailing. And wail they did. Soon, the compound was filled. Half of the villagers gathered together, crying with my mother, while calling the names of their own deceased relatives. After several hours of crying, the exhausted villagers dispersed little by little. Their mission was accomplished: to weep with those who wept.

My mother felt she couldn't grieve any longer than that one night because she needed to keep making money for her family. Consequently, she began to encourage P-to-P again.

The next day, my mother showed P-to-P the flour and other baking ingredients that her second son, Sheik, had given her. "Your brother believed in you and in your dreams. Make him proud."

P-to-P was incredibly excited and leapt into action. But he had never baked before. And, well, the internet or YouTube was not a thing then. How would he launch his dream of running a bakery with zero skills?

Ever heard of trial and error? Well, that's exactly what he did. P-to-P simply began pouring things and mixing them together. He trusted and depended only on his intuition. He would randomly pour yeast and flour in specific quantities and mix them in a bowl. As you can guess quite correctly, it was not a pleasant sight.

Sometimes, there would be too much water, and at other times, too little. Time and time again, the mixtures had to be thrown away. But P-to-P was baking with his deceased brother in mind. It spurred him on.

This trial and error went on for many weeks, consecutively. And then the tiny seeds of frustration began to sprout. The ingredients were dwindling with each trial, and he was nowhere close to anything that smelled like success. In fact, there was little or no progress at all.

He was on the verge of giving up when Samba, the native doctor who had healed him, was visiting a neighbouring village, and decided to pass by Madina. That was when light appeared at the end of the dark tunnel. The doctor came to learn about his baking dream and his unfortunate trials and errors.

"I know a man who might be able to show you how to mix and bake," he suggested.

This man, who had been in Freetown before and now in a neighbouring village, had been baking for several years and soon began to send tips and instructions to P-to-P through Samba. The more tips he received, the more P-to-P's confidence grew.

However, his two bags of flour had almost run out before he could even try to hone his efforts. Again, Samba stepped in and promised to organize flour for

P-to-P to perfect his training.

Two weeks after Samba's departure from Madina, one evening, P-to-P received a message that there was a package waiting for him at the junction. There was something he needed to collect from the Poda Poda driver before he left. You would not believe what he saw. Sitting in a corner, tied in sacks, were four bags of flour sent to him by Samba. That day, he and Diamond danced under the rain in celebration of the gifts he had received.

The very next day, without further ado, he began his baking career. The first real bread he made had his initials, P-to-P, stamped on it. When the bread was baked, he presented it to my mother.

"Mama, I made this for you," he said, beaming with pride. It was a big loaf of bread, but it was not fully baked inside. P-to-P was far from being deterred. "Tomorrow will be better," he said enthusiastically.

He kept baking until he was baking one or two dozen loaves of bread every day and even gave some to the neighbours. The neighbours spread the word. His bread was delicious and had a signature name. P-to-P soon became a popular young man in the village.

He eventually decided to start selling the bread, rather than only giving them out for free. If a buyer did not have cash in hand, they could trade with a young goat or a sheep for a few days of bread supply. P-to-P never attended school, but somehow, he made a sign using palm tree leaves to spell out his famous name, P-to-P, and hung it in front of the bakery. In less than no time, he had quickly gathered enough goats, sheep, and even cows to create a cattle farm.

Diamond was responsible for selling the loaves of bread to the neighbouring villages. She would carry the freshly baked bread in a big basket and walk three or four hours to the surrounding towns. Most times, she would return with an empty basket. This was how much my people loved bread. Whether with palm oil or beans, this bread recipe was famous in Sierra Leone.

Things were steadily improving, almost as much as the time my mother sold palm oil. We had a farm and a budding bakery business. Maybe the storm was finally over, and the rainbows could finally come out.

But there was a slight problem: None of us could

accurately forecast the weather. We couldn't know for sure if the storm was really over.

This is what life had been like so far for the fast-growing Bangura family. It seemed like we were always shifting from one chaotic situation to the next, and somehow still managed to survive it all. Each time life threw its worst lemons at us, we made the best lemonade and kept going. It was little wonder that soon, we would once again become one of the most respectable families in the whole of Madina.

CHAPTER 5

June 1989: The Storyteller is Born

Life in the Bangura family was pretty uneventful after this period. The main event that happened was my birth.

As I've mentioned, I am child number 24, and I was the last child of the Bangura family. After my birth, there were no more children from either woman. To call me God's plan would not be far from the truth. You see, my birth is just the steppingstone into a deeper story than the one you've been told from the beginning of this book.

I am the storyteller, and this is my voice. This is my story and my mission. I'm going to take you back to the labour room in the backyard of the most reputable midwife in Madina, and my mother's grapple with death that followed my entry into this world.

It was a rainy Tuesday morning when my mother began to feel pain. She was pregnant with me. At around lunchtime, the contractions had become severe, causing her long bouts of agony. As my mother later told me, the pains she experienced that day were the worst ones of her entire life. Apparently, I gave her the hardest time of all her deliveries. After having birthed several children before me, she thought there was nothing she couldn't handle.

Around 4 pm that evening in the midwife's house, she passed out from the pain. The midwife quickly sent a message to the family, who, in turn, reached out to Samba in Macassa—who had become a family friend—about my mother's critical condition. Samba was no specialist when it came to childbirth.

Everyone quickly assumed that birth complications meant there was something supernatural about the pregnancy. It could be witchcraft or a spell, they would say, hence the need for Samba to be present. It was assumed that he would see things the midwife could not see and save my mother from dying.

Just as a messenger was dispatched to fetch him, urgent news arrived from Freetown to the family in Madina. My mother's first daughter, Abbigail, had just gotten married and would be travelling overseas in the coming week. No one saw that coming. A black man, Amara, who had moved abroad, had just come back to visit his family. My sister, Abbigail, had caught his fancy.

It was love at first sight for Amara, if you believe in such things. He was sitting outside of one of the most beautiful units near Gorey Street when he spotted Abbigail passing by with her friend. Abbigail was tall, bubbly, and had an infectious smile that was even further complemented by a billion-dollar body. And

Amara, well, he was just an average man who had the opportunity to travel overseas. He was too shy to approach her himself and had simply whispered to his people, "That's the girl I would like to marry."

Amara's family immediately went to see Father and informed him of their son's intentions to marry my sister. Abbigail flat out rejected the proposal. It took Father weeks of persuasion to get my sister to even agree to look at the poor man.

"This is an opportunity for my daughter. It could change the Bangura family forever," Father said. When he saw his efforts were futile, Father had finally pulled the ultimate trick—he guilt tripped Abbigail. He reminded her of how many younger siblings looked up to her and told her that the destiny of the Bangura family was in her hands. Someone could have argued that Father chose to see positive in this situation.

That did the trick. Abbigail finally agreed to marry Amara. She requested to travel to Madina to see my mother, but due to Amara's visa situation, they had to leave almost immediately. There were several papers to organize for that, so the visit to my mother was cancelled.

A week later, Father and Elder Mama said goodbye to Abbigail as she and her husband departed for the airport.

Back in Madina, my mother was still struggling for her life. After a lot of fanning, native medications, and prayers, she finally regained consciousness. But her situation was still very critical. At this point, she had already begun to give up.

"I...I don't think I can...make it. Ple–please look after my children for me..." she whispered to the ladies rallying around her in the labour room. Everyone began to sob.

At 10 pm, Samba arrived. He went straight into a room and wrote something on a plank of wood using a tiny bamboo stick shaped like a pen. The writing was washed off with water into a bowl and he brought the dark liquid next door for my mother to drink to ease her pain. Meanwhile, the elderly ladies were still desperately trying to save both my mother and me.

At 11:59 pm on 19 June, my mother pushed one last

big push. And just as the clock ticked 12 am on 20 June 1989, my mother's eighth son (and the 24th child between the two families) was born!

But the pandemonium was far from over. Immediately after giving birth, my mother began to lose consciousness again. Hours of struggling and severe pain had taken a toll on her.

"Wh-what is happening? I can't see anyone. I can't feel any parts of my body," my mother said as she struggled to stay awake, her words barely audible.

This sent the women into another frenzy of panic. They did not know whether to cry, run, or continue to try to save this woman who was a mother to so many children. As morning came, the tension in the air grew. It had taken everyone until the break of dawn to realise how long this had been going on. As reality set in, some of the ladies began shaking and crying. Everyone was exhausted and terrified. Most importantly, everyone had run out of ideas about what to do. A hospital or clinic was out of question. This dark backroom of the most reputable midwife in Madina was the top hospital around—no more, no less. My mother was—and still is—a fighter.

By sunset on June 21, 1989, my mother won the battle and gradually regained awareness of her surroundings. As soon as she could talk, her first words were, "Where is my baby boy?"

The universe unfolded as it should. Three years into this world, I was forced to end my childhood in order to survive. What unfolded next led me to learn about loss and death way before I could spell correctly.

CHAPTER 6

Sierra Leone: The Diamond Land

Sierra Leone was popularly known as Salone, meaning 'Roaring Mountain' in Portuguese. The name was coined by the Portuguese explorer, Pedro da Cintra, upon seeing the country's mountainous terrain. Apart from our land being famous for our minerals, especially diamonds, we host a variety of rich cultures, all living harmoniously alongside each other, according to stories my mother told me.

The eleven-year civil war in Sierra Leone was centred around the country's rich mineral resources, particularly diamonds, which later came to be known as *blood diamonds*. They were referred to as *blood diamonds* because of the atrocities committed to obtain them. Our people were brainwashed into taking up arms against the government and fellow citizens with the promise of a better life.

For 11 years, our people were slaughtered, and families were torn apart. Kids were taken from the bosoms of their mothers, given drugs, and forced to harm their family members and loved ones. They were brainwashed into participating in hate crimes against civilians and were welcomed back as heroes among the rebels. The more heinous the act, the better the rebel leaders treated them; they were often given command and authority as rewards. As a result of these acts, these kids were marginalised by their family members. They had no one to turn to but the rebels for help and protection. This was a strategy implemented by the RUF (Rebel United Front) because they knew the opposition would hesitate to kill children. During the war, children were the greatest weapons and shields. All these atrocities inflicted on our people have resulted in more than 90% of the general population experiencing a form of mental illness, particularly Post Traumatic Stress Disorder (PTSD).

The president of the neighbouring country fuelled the war in return for our diamonds. Years after the war, he was later prosecuted for his war crimes. To this day, his name brings great fear to our people.

As I stated from the beginning, my father was a diamond digger. It was all he knew how to do. He migrated to the Kono districts in pursuit of diamonds and spent his time building mining groups to search for and mine these precious stones. On the 20th of April in 1978, the 14th child was born, Diamond. She was the child whose birth had brought Father one of the biggest diamonds in Kono at that time.

From the stories my parents told me, my country was a beautiful and peaceful place then. We were very united and didn't care much about things like politics.

We had a chief and some elders, and that was enough for us.

But, like every country with an abundance of natural resources and reserves, we were open to exploitation and manipulation. We had foreigners come in frequently and businesses were established. This led to the rise of our economy and subsequently selfishness and greed. With growth came a price we sadly had to pay, and it came at the cost of the blood of the people.

The saddest part of the events to follow was the fact that no one saw it coming. Or at least no one had imagined it would last that long or would be that bloody.

As for the Bangura family, nothing prepared us for the amount of loss we would suffer. There was strength in numbers, but not in our case. The size of our family meant it was almost impossible to stay together. We were 24 children and three adults! How do you keep 27 people together? We couldn't stay together, not unless someone built an underground bunker and housed us all below. There was no such thing. It would be every man for himself and that would be one of our greatest weaknesses.

I was just a child happy to be born. A child without any clue that this world I was born into had no mercy for children and that it would be hard to even survive!

The civil war started in 1991. The same year my sister, Salamatu, had her first child, Shishi, while still living with my uncle, Thaimu Bangura, in Freetown. I was but a child. I was barely three years old and knew nothing about the war or what effects it would have on me. The older I grew, the closer to the front lines I drew, and the more exposure to trauma I got.

By age three, I began to comprehend the impact of the war around me. With my sparkly, curious eyes, I would look up at my mother and ask her why everywhere was always noisy and why we stayed indoors, or why we ran into the forest so often.

With a worried look on her face, she would hush me and say everything would be alright. But everything was not alright. In fact, everything got worse.

Soon, the war began to spread from the big towns to the small villages and, eventually, it found the capital, Freetown. Opposition sparked here and there, and several blood-thirsty rebel groups began to form. These rebels were not seeking volunteers to join their movement. Instead, they forcefully recruited young boys and killed those who refused. It was a do or die mission.

At one point, it was so dangerous to remain in our village, Madina, that the 23rd child, Musa, and I had to flee to Macassa to live with Samba, his three wives, and two children, Sally and Alpha. Samba's family accommodated us like one of their own and even told us that the man in the house was our father. I was five years old at that time and it was a very perplexing situation for me. The face of the man I had called my father was different from the face of the new man who was introduced to me as my father.

Who, then, was really my father? I could not hold it in anymore. One day, when my mother came to join us, I asked her straight to her face.

"Is it true, Mama? Is he our father?"

"No. He is not your father. He is an old friend," my mother replied. And that answer calmed my young, confused mind.

I was especially close to Musa. We were not far apart in age, unlike my numerous elder siblings who towered above me with really large age gaps. Musa looked after me pretty well and he was the one I ran to whenever I had questions.

In Macassa, we adapted pretty quickly to life with the friendly man who we began to call Father. At 4:30 am, we would get up to begin preparations to go to the farm. Whether it was dry or raining, to the farm we went. It was five miles away from our house, so we had to get up early to reach the site on time. One of our major problems at the farm back then were pests. It was a rice farm and birds liked to lurk around. Musa, Alpha, and I decided to improvise a solution.

At first, we would lose our voices after spending all day yelling at the birds to scare them off. Therefore, together, we created instruments to help scare the birds away. This instrument was able to produce several musical notes. We usually made the keys from wood, which was dried slowly over a low flame. The excess wood was then trimmed from underneath the keys with small gourds created to amplify them. To flatten or sharpen the keys, we hollowed out the middle. This instrument looked like a xylophone and made buzzing, hollow noises loud enough to scare the birds away and entertain us at the same time.

When it was time for lunch, Alpha would go hunting while we continued with the party and scaring the birds away. He would return with bush meat, cassava, and bush yam. We would boil the cassava together with the meat, sprinkle some salt on it, wrap it with banana leaves, and bury it while applying heat to the top. Those were simple, happy times, that strengthened my bond with Musa considerably. We didn't have a single care in the world. We were just two young boys in the woods who were glad to have each other's company.

Once dusk settled, we would begin to make our journey back home with bare feet and our arms draped over each other's shoulders. We whistled together or hummed random tunes. It was all we knew and all we had.

As an adult now, I realise that Sierra Leone is a unique country where people can coexist in peace despite race or religion. Our beaches are world famous due to their impeccable beauty and luscious, white, clean sand that grinds under your feet when you walk. Sierra Leonians are particularly fond of foreigners and are quite welcoming. Visitors are treated like kings and queens.

CHAPTER 7

My Vow to my Mother and Musa

Out of all my siblings, there was no one I loved and cared for more than Musa, and vice versa. Perhaps it was because he was my immediate elder brother, or it was due to the fact that we spent more time in each other's company—I do not know for sure. All I know is that we were practically inseparable. Little did we know that, very soon, this bond would be tested severely.

This beloved brother of mine had a serious health condition. He was always experiencing moments of unconsciousness and violent muscle contractions that came frequently and suddenly. As a kid, I never really understood what was wrong, but I was smart enough to realise that my brother's condition was not normal and that it caused him unimaginable pain. Thinking positively during these hard times was like asking me to read with my eyes closed.

When the contractions came, he would begin to roll about with such force and without any direction. He would get seriously injured if there was no one around to hold him still. Even though I had no idea what caused his condition, I tried my best to be more observant than the rest of my family members. Over time, I was able to notice when the contractions were about to begin. I always held him steady even though he was larger in size than I was. Each time the episodes came, I felt his pain in my little heart and resolved within myself that I would care for this brother of mine with all I had.

It wasn't until adulthood that I came to learn that his condition had a name. It was called Chronic Tonic Seizure Condition. With my brother's severe condition, a new love was birthed. I love him more than words can describe.

A couple of dry and rainy seasons had passed, yet things became no better. Musa's condition kept deteriorating. By this time, we were at the end of primary school. They say adversity introduces a man to himself, and it does—but I was not a man. I was still a boy. I had to stop going to school to look after my brother. His seizures had become more frequent. At this stage, I had to assume full caregiver responsibilities of my brother, Musa, even though I was still a child myself.

As for my mother, she was not always around. She had to frequently travel back and forth to see Father, who was no longer the able-bodied man he used to be. Elder Mama stayed in Freetown.

You see, in Sierra Leone, the man was the primary breadwinner of the family. His worth or value as a man was measured by how well he was able to care for his household. It didn't matter if circumstances were beyond his control or if things suddenly went downhill. It was up to him as the man of the house to manage and still provide chop money to feed the family.

Boys were raised to continue this cycle and priority was given to raising a male child who could shoulder the responsibilities of manhood without complaining, breaking down, or opening up about their struggles. Men who did those things were stereotyped as weak males and were used as a negative example by others in the community. Their wives gave them no respect and sometimes even their children took them for granted. A man's pride was in being able to raise his shoulders high even if everything inside him was falling apart.

With this mindset, my father, who was once a hardworking man, was distraught at the sudden twist of events that left him penniless. He was a man who was proud of the labour and sweat it took to mine diamonds. Now, he was without the ability to care for his large family of 24 children.

As the looming war intensified and spread to the villages and smaller communities, Father's chances of recovering from his plunge into joblessness continued to dwindle. The mining business had collapsed, and a few menial jobs had not been enough to sustain the household. In a bid to survive, Father had once swallowed his pride and sold off his car and our big house in the city. Some of my brothers had been given off as menpikins and others were scattered around in different communities. Some also stayed with a few relatives.

Slowly but surely, Father began to withdraw into depression. We didn't know what it was back then; we simply thought he was aging or getting sick. Before our eyes, he went from being a man full of life to barely managing to get through a single day.

Although my mother worked twice as hard to support him, it was never enough. He could not provide for his family, and his children had to suffer for it. Whatever menial jobs he could find, he did. As time went on, things got even worse for my father. He could barely eat and began to look very pale and sickly. There was something about Father's eyes. He was an alert man. His eyes noticed everything and seemed to have wisdom in them. When we were kids, a stern look from our father was enough to get everyone in order.

But as my mother said later, his eyes began to lose their touch. He was less alert and often absent minded. He was always deep in thought and mumbled to himself. Days turned into weeks and weeks into months, and our father's condition continued to deteriorate. At one point, he could no longer go out to find menial jobs. Sheik and Haji, my elder brothers, had to look after him. My mother and Elder Mama's first daughter, Cynthia, helped look after him, as well.

Due to our poor financial situation, going to the hospital was as impossible as getting a camel to give birth to a bird. We could only afford to give him home treatments and pray for a miracle. But a miracle did not happen. Everyone knew something was wrong, but nobody could figure out what that was.

My mother, my brother, Sheik, and Cynthia continued to provide care for him at home. Then one day, as everyone was seated in the big parlour room, Father suddenly got up and started screaming and yelling that he wanted to leave this world. Everyone, including the neighbours, gathered around him and tried to console him, but he continued to be hysterical all morning.

When he eventually calmed down, he went to his room and, according to my mother, he just stared wide eyed at the ceiling. He stayed like that the entire day. He refused food, drink, and any other form of comfort. He did not even respond to his family when they called his name. The scene outside the room was chaotic. It was like a zombie movie, only this time, it involved real people.

As always, a crowd gathered outside our house and everyone in attendance was teary eyed. The elders were gathered in a corner of the living room whispering in hushed voices, the women were inconsolable, and the kids ran wild.

My mother later said she thought for sure my father was going to die that day. She had felt it so strongly that when a messenger came bearing grave news of Musa's illness, she had burst out weeping that she was going to lose two people at once.

With the arrival of this news, she had to make a very tough decision. Two important people in her life were on the brink of death. Who would she choose to be with?

In the end, Father persuaded my mother to make up her mind. Father had been firm in his insistence. My mother would go to her son.

With a heavy heart, thinking this might be the last time she ever saw her husband, my mother packed a small bag prepared to make the journey to Macassa, to Musa and me.

As she began her silent, sombre journey, she felt her heart break into several pieces. The thoughts of her ailing husband and son overwhelmed her.

It took my mother one month to return to Father. Musa's Tonic Chronic Seizure Condition had been very long and terrible, but he survived it. As for Father, his condition had gotten much worse. Everyone was on edge and afraid of what they knew would happen soon.

While recounting the events of that time, my mother told us she remembered returning to my father's bedside to see a pale man. Seeing him again brought a fresh wave of sadness over her.

She had returned to meet a nearly lifeless form that was once vibrant and the head of our large family. He was almost unrecognizable. There was no trace of a smile on his face and his cheekbones looked sharp, as if they wanted to protrude from his skin each time he tried to catch a breath. Every time my mother recounts this story, I feel nauseated.

I cannot quite describe the way I felt when Father died. We were far from each other. He was in Freetown, and I was in Macassa, yet it felt like I was there. It felt like I was in that very room where a few of my brothers and our mothers had gathered. This man was my father. I had barely spent time with him since Musa and I had been away for so long, but still, I admired him greatly. My boyish heart could not understand how he changed from the superman I thought he was, into the weak, white-haired, breathless man who now lay helplessly in bed.

That day in that room, time seemed to stop. Even the animals stayed quiet. The only sounds were my father's heavy gasps for air and my family breathing. My siblings entered and exited the room throughout the day, each with gloomy expressions and red eyes. His wives sat on either side of his bed, fanning him. Even though his breathing was shallow and laboured, his vacant eyes still stared around the room.

I was still looking after Musa in Macassa during this heartbreaking moment for my family. Even though I was not present, I felt the pain so strongly. I could only wonder how terrible it would have been to watch my father take his last dying breaths.

That day, I felt sick, and my heart seemed heavy with sadness. I had no idea where it came from. The saying, 'Blood is thicker than water,' was so true; Father and I shared a special connection.

I later shared with my mother that, during the evening around the time Father had died, I felt a sudden, strong stab of pain clutch at my heart.

It was like someone had taken a knife and was stabbing me repeatedly with it.

There was no explanation for why I felt that way.

Yet, Musa's repeated attempts to console me and ease my pain proved futile. Something very deeply connected to me had gone and my body was reacting to the loss.

When word came to us the next day that my father had died the previous day, everything suddenly made sense. The head of our family was gone, and I had gotten the signals. For a long time, I uttered no word as I allowed the messenger's grave news sink into my soul.

Then, in one hysterical impulsive reaction, I burst out screaming.

"My heart hurts—everything hurts," I began. My young heart mourned for the father I never got a chance to spend much time with. The man who had told me stories of conquests, diamonds, and fast cars. The undefeatable hero who I had so often wanted to be like was gone. It was then that I felt my feet give way and darkness overtook my consciousness.

I later learned from my brother that I had collapsed then and there. I had one burning desire in my mind. I was a still a child, but I felt this strong determination course through my bones and fill me up with an unimaginable passion. I would take care of my mother and make my father proud. That was my vow.

Back to my responsibilities. It was Friday evening, and everyone had just arrived home from the farm. Musa was standing near the stairs looking very confused. His eyes had a distant look in them, and I knew what that meant. He was about to have one of his episodes. My entire body went on full alert. I knew his episodes even better than he did, so I was prepared for what would happen next.

He broke into a sprint and I, already on alert mode, dashed after him. Now, the thing with Musa was that whenever he was about to go into one of his episodes, he suddenly had superhuman strength. He was hard to catch and even harder to control. Sprinting like we were in a relay race, I finally caught up with him after several meters. He dropped to the concrete floor, motionless like a heavy sack of rice. I could see blood spraying like a fountain from his left ear and the grim sight threw me off balance for a few seconds. Once I recovered, I knelt by his side, cradled his head in my arms, and screamed for help as the seizures thrashed him about very violently. My brother was in pain, and I could only cry helplessly as I rocked his body while praying for the seizures to subside. It was not a pretty sight. I still struggle to get over those ugly memories to this day.

The war had taken over the whole country and people were always hiding. As a child, I had learnt very early how to respond quickly to signals that meant we had to hide, like the sound of cars, motorbikes, or footsteps. But for Musa, this was a struggle. You see, hiding meant we had to keep as quiet as possible. And Musa, who still battled with his seizures, screamed very loudly during those episodes. Whenever we were in hiding, everyone would try to avoid staying in close proximity to us for fear of Musa suddenly having an episode. I could not blame them though, for Musa's screams were loud enough to reveal our location to the rebels and that would mean death for anyone who was found. Who would want to be a part of that?

When my mother was around, the situation was often different. We would be allowed to hide with everyone else. But when she wasn't, we were on our own. We were segregated by everyone else and had to protect and fend for ourselves. Often, we had to go into hiding, just the two of us, because no one wanted us to compromise their location.

I could not leave my brother no matter how loudly he screamed. After each seizure, he would tearfully thank me for being with him. Sometimes, when we had to hide alone for days, we would get so hungry that our only option was to eat grass or starve. We didn't have to think twice. We gladly munched on grass until we could come out of hiding and reunite with others.

It was 1998, seven years into the war. Now, picture this scenario. Two brothers who were scared and alone, one aged ten and the other aged nine, hiding in the dark, hungry and exhausted for days. Not just that, but the elder brother was sick and had to be looked after by his little brother. That was us! That was the condition we found ourselves in, and somehow, we managed to survive every single time—but not without a few mishaps.

A year later, in 1999, to our family's dismay, my uncle, Thaimu Bangura, died.

During these times, the sound of gunshots and the

smell of gunpowder were the two things with which we were most familiar. Smoke from villages being set on fire and burning huts and vehicles, and the screams from children being captured were the order of the day. The sound of wailing mothers and the loud, terrorizing voices of rebel soldiers as they chased their victims were all too familiar to us—so much so that we could even hear them in our sleep.

On some days, the sky was bright and clear, and then suddenly, the rebels would attack. They would burn huts and abduct young boys. They fired bullets without a specific target in mind. You either ducked or got hit. In those moments of utter terror, the sky would be a dark reddish-brown, or sometimes grey, depending on how thick the smoke was from the burning villages. As children, the red sky often fascinated us. Even though its colour meant doom and ashes, there was just something beautiful about lying down in the bush as we hid and watched the sky light up with explosions from gunshots. These were our fireworks.

At times, if we were still in the village when the explosions began, we would cough our way through the entire event, careful not to be too loud as we made our way to our hideouts. Sometimes we ran blindly, unable to see where we were going in the thick smoke. We ran forward regardless and let fear guide our feet.

When the rebels were gone and we could finally come out, the air would smell like burnt wood. We would gather whatever remained; mothers sobbed as they held their children close. The men watched helplessly. Only the older people seemed to understand the gravity of our situation. As for the children, we were simply glad to be out of the hideout, which had less air and very little space to accommodate the crowd that sought shelter in it.

One showery July evening in 1999 during the rainy season, I sat on the ground leaning on one of the roots underneath a humungous tree. Musa was unconscious from a seizure and had his head on my lap. We were alone together as usual, having been cast out again. Suddenly, I noticed a 30-foot, bulky snake with a triangular head. I could not move. Musa was still unconscious. If we made any sudden movements, we could be the snake's dinner.

Rain poured as we sat under the tree. My tiny body was soaked to the core from the rain and other bodily fluids. My hands were trembling—not from the cold, but from the fear of knowing that we had a very slim chance of escaping the huge snake. I sat still, held my breath, and prayed that somehow a miracle would happen. Thankfully, Musa regained consciousness very quickly and I covered his mouth with one hand as soon as his eyes popped open. With my other free hand, I gestured to the huge python that was circling us a few meters from where we sat. Slowly, and as carefully as we could, we crawled up to our feet, backed away, doubled our steps, and ran away as fast as possible.

On other occasions, when Musa was well and conscious and we were segregated from the villagers, I remember combing our way through the bushes, scared, alone, and hungry. We crouched low, with our knees almost touching the bare soil, as we made our way deeper into the bushes where we were sure the rebel soldiers could not find us. The thick forest served to protect us during such times, but not when it rained. For when the rains came, crouching low caused any of the angry forest animals to panic and attack. As the gunshots rang through our ears, and the occasional explosions sounded, our hearts sank deeper with each step we took into the forest. A stray bullet could find you even in the bush, and if it didn't, then the animals might.

A few weeks later, my mother returned to us. When we heard the rebels were coming again, the whole village ran to the usual hiding spots. This time, we were allowed to hide with everyone else. While we were hiding, Musa had an episode where he got up and ran. Before anyone could get to him, he fell on top of a freshly cut tree and was stabbed through the thigh by a pointy, protruding piece of the tree stump. My mother and I went to him, took it out of his leg, and tried to stop the bleeding. We just held each other after that and cried.

While back in hiding, a man who was with us caught a huge python. Our thoughts wandered back to the encounter we had with a snake on that rainy day in the bush. Could it be the same python? We knew not. The point was that snake meat was here and everyone was dancing and rejoicing. We had not seen meat for months, and this was enough to be grateful for.

Like my mother always said, you had to be grateful and thankful for what you had and how far you came. When I was young, I never understood why she was always resolved when saying this, but now I realise what she meant.

Back then, our life was a game. You woke up and didn't even know if you would see the next sunset. It was us versus the rebels and I learned how to sleep with one eye open. The adults stayed awake in groups and took turns listening for the signal that meant the rebels were coming. It was the sound of footsteps, a car, or a motor bike sound that signalled this because only the rebels could use any means of transportation. One call and everyone—adult or child—would dash into the bushes and make a beeline for our hiding spots. It was either this or death.

What a childhood! This was my reality. It was the life of many children during the ugly Sierra Leonean Civil War. It was the reality that robbed us of the joys of what childhood could have been. The reality that forced us to learn survival before we could count. I would come to learn that there would be plenty of sacrifices in war. Sacrifices I was never prepared to make.

CHAPTER 8

The Sound of War and Loss

They say the stench of war is one that does not easily go away. I say the scars are greater. But neither the stench nor the scars can be compared to the heavy choice of saving oneself at the expense of a loved one. You have to weigh the choice so carefully—to lose one or to lose all. And in the end, no matter how justifiable the sacrifice was, making the sacrifice is a heavy cross for the surviving party to bear.

Musa and I were always together. Wherever Musa was, you would find me. Even with his sickness, he was never boring company. Though we never said it out loud to each other, I loved my brother fiercely and he loved me the same. Along with that love came a strong sense of loyalty. I never complained when I had to look after him, nor did I ever think of leaving his side when the seizures came. I knew he would do the same for me if he were in my shoes.

Months had passed and Samba and my mother decided to get married. This was a huge decision for my mother, but it was one that Musa and I supported. This man had been nothing but good to us. Since I didn't have the opportunity to spend much time with my father, Samba was like a father to me.

The cold hands of the war continued to gain on us, but I had yet to experience my first life-and-death situation. I didn't have to wait long.

It was around 8 pm in the village and the moon was out, shining brightly. Musa and I were living with my mother and Samba at Macassa.

We were thankful to have seen another sunset and

were getting ready to eat dinner. Dinner consisted of whatever the adults could get their hands on. We never really cared for what we ate. Whatever was given to us in the bowl or plate, we ate and thanked the heavens that we didn't have to starve that day.

On this fateful day, all the elders had gathered around the fireplace after dinner and the kids played in groups. Our dinner for that day was roasted cassava—a favourite of every child in the village. The moon was out, and the night sky looked beautiful. The air around us was crisp and smelled warm and inviting. The aroma from the roasted cassavas was a delight to inhale. The men shared stories as they took turns poking the fire and roasting the cassava. There was something yummy about the smell of the wood and cassava as it roasted together. The aroma filled everyone with an instant appetite. Even though we were delighted to be together, everyone was on alert as usual, and ready to run at the smallest noise.

The adults and children celebrated another day of being alive. It was on this day, as I was playing with some of the other kids around the fire, that Musa informed me he needed to use the toilet.

The toilet was in a bushy location, about one km from the village so the smell wouldn't reach the village. I had to escort him there, of course. On our way, we collected the finest leaves that were big enough to serve as tissue paper. The irony of these leaves was that it didn't matter how good they looked or how big they were in size. From time to time, your fingers would be sure to poke through the foliage straight into your butt.

I'm sure kids of this generation would say, 'Eww, disgusting, ughh ...' and more at the thought of having to do such a thing. But for us, it was the most normal thing to do. It was either that or have the left-over faeces on your anus.

I think we must have been gone for nearly 40 minutes. When we returned to the village, it dawned on us that something was very wrong. It was quiet—too quiet. And cold. The fireplace was gone! It had been watered off and everything seemed to have been done in a hurry.

Oh no! Everyone had gone into hiding. Musa and I turned to each other at the same time as the realisation hit us. Before we could turn to look for a place to hide, a woman stepped out of the shadows.

We realised too late that she was a female rebel. *So, the rebels recruited women, too. Ah!* No one had told us that.

With our hearts beating rapidly out of fear and cold sweat drenching our bodies, she told us that she would take us as rebel soldiers. Musa was quick to dramatically inform her that he was sick. She paused for a while, as if examining him with her eyes, and then turned her attention to me.

"I am sick, too!" I blurted out without thinking. It was the only response my brain could come up with. She could tell right away that I was lying. My eyes focused on her, and I watched her put the gun across her shoulder so she could grab me.

I had been sprinting almost all my life. From running to catch Musa whenever his episodes began, to running to our hiding spot whenever we heard the rebels coming. It was almost as if I had been training for this moment.

Before she could grab me, I glanced towards Musa and our eyes met. We knew what we had to do. Sprinting like deer, we both dashed away, the adrenaline fuelling our pace. As we ran, I shouted my mother's name, hoping she would come save us from our pursuer, the rebel soldier. In our native tongue, I was practically screaming. "Mama! Mama! *Ar k ra me*! Please come and help us! The rebels...they want to take us away! Mama!" There was silence.

I shouted repeatedly, not slowing my pace one bit as we ran into the bushes. But there was no response. I could only hear the night insects chirping away and the sound of our bare feet tapping forcefully on the hard earth that echoed back. We had no clue where we were running, but somehow, we both managed to run in unison in the same direction.

My mother was my saviour. She always saved us from any situation; she was our own superwoman. *Surely, she will come out and take us to safety*, I thought. We collapsed on the dry leaves in the forest and as I took a deep breath, I looked at my brother and thought, *This is it! This is how we end.*

Thankfully, our pursuer gave up the chase. It could be that she suddenly decided she had better things to do than pursue two little boys in the dark bushes. Whatever it was that made her turn back, Musa and I were grateful for that, for we feared we couldn't keep running, and that would have meant death, at least for one of us.

Even though our pursuer was long gone, we did not stop running. We rose to our feet and ran and ran until our little legs gave out. Then, we collapsed with each other on a small bush full of dry leaves until dawn came.

When morning arrived, Musa and I began the long walk back to the village where we finally reunited with our mother. With tears bubbling in her eyes, she squeezed us tightly in her embrace and profusely apologised to us.

It didn't take long for me to realise why my mother was apologising. She had heard us last night. She had heard my desperate cry for help. But if she had stepped out that night, she would have been killed instantly. That was my first personal encounter with a life-and-death situation at the hands of the rebel soldiers. And in my young nine-year-old mind, it left a memory I would never forget.

In April, the end of the dry season, our life in Macassa was becoming overwhelming and my mother was tired of having to travel to and from Madina and having to leave us. So, we decided to return to Madina with her, and we were reunited with P-to-P.

One night during this month, Samba came to check how we were doing in Madina. I overheard him vowing to my mother that he would continue to come and check on us regularly henceforth. He would stay this time for a week and then return to Macassa to his other family.

My young mind often replayed the events of the night Musa and I had almost been caught. I remembered how desperate I had been to receive my mother's help, and I remembered how disheartened I felt when I realised that my mother could not always protect us.

I would *keep* running and hiding. If that was what it took to stay alive, I would do it. And just like that night had taught me that there wasn't much anyone could do to protect me. It was every man for himself.

A few days after our arrival in Madina, we received news that the 18th child, Baida, my sister from my mother's side, had been captured by the rebels and that they were going to kill her. The family was in turmoil. Even though I didn't know this sister of mine, the fact that she was captured by rebel soldiers was enough to make me feel some pain. No one wished capture on their enemies, let alone a family member. But the family did not have to worry about Baida for long. Soon, she was rescued by Ismalie, a rebel who put his life on the line for her. Ismalie had fallen in love with Baida at first sight. He acted as a guarantor and promised to take care of her. If she should escape, he would be killed. So, Baida was Ismalie's responsibility now. He saw to it that she was protected and well taken care of as his own captive.

However, life had other plans for them. During the captive and master arrangement, Baida also developed feelings for him and fell in love. This was the beginning of a risky and forbidden affair that could ultimately lead to their deaths if anyone in the rebel camp found out. Only the leader of the rebel camp was above any law.

After secretly dating for months, Baida became pregnant. It was at this point that Ismalie had to make a major decision. They would flee from the camp. It was the only way they could both stay alive and even have a chance of continuing their love affair.

For days, they travelled through rivers and forests, eating only peanuts and whatever the forest provided. Finally, they travelled to another village far away from the rebel's camp and began to live as ordinary civilians. It was there, in that village, that their daughter was born.

I can still remember very vividly the events that would soon unfold, for in one swift moment, we would experience our first loss brought by the war. The loss of the pillar of our family.

One Friday evening, just as the first streaks of the sun began to set, the rebels launched a surprise attack. They parked their cars three km away from the village and snuck up on the ever-alert villagers by travelling on foot in disguise.

I woke up to the sounds of screams. There had been no signal call to indicate that we should start running. It was a complete surprise.

Our house was on fire. Not just ours, but several other houses, too. Everyone was trapped inside as thick smoke engulfed the entire building. All the children began to cry and shout at the same time. We could barely see anything through the smoke and our parents were nowhere to be found.

Finally, Samba came into our room through the smoke, coughing and trying to usher us out of the building. The doors were blocked, and our exits were limited. We couldn't breathe properly because of the thick smoke.

He managed to get me, my mother, P-to-P, and Musa out of the building before we heard more explosions. Our entire bodies were covered in soot and Musa was in a terrible condition. Once he had made sure we were a safe distance away, Samba turned around to go back to the raging inferno that was once our house.

My mother was tearful as she tried to stop him, and

we all followed suit, begging him to stay.

"I have to try to collect all important documents and the little money we have saved," he began.

My mother desperately urged him to forget everything, her voice hoarse from the smoke. But he was determined to return. "What about the other families still trapped inside? We can't abandon them," he pleaded. My mother knew this time that there was nothing she could say. She wailed even more.

He asked us to run into the bushes to hide and wait for him. "I will be back soon," he promised, with tears in his eyes. My mother broke down into a bitter sob. All the children cried as we gathered around to comfort her. I watched him rush back towards the burning building to help other families.

As he approached the fire, he turned back and screamed at us to go further into the bushes and reassured us that he would meet up with us later when everyone was out. I'll never forget how brave I thought he was as I watched him disappear into the burning building. A few minutes later, from a distance in the bush, we watched with heavy hearts, and listened to my mother's heartbreaking scream, as the walls of the building collapsed.

In a matter of seconds, the whole building crumbled into a huge heap, with the remains of my dear hero were buried along with it.

None of us slept a wink that night. We just sat with each other, sobbing quietly, mourning and comforting each other. I was just ten years old when I watched Samba, my hero, die.

With no time to grieve, and no way of letting his other family know, P-to-P, Musa, my mother, and I continued to run for our lives from one town to the next for weeks. The war was getting worse, and more villages were destroyed and burnt down. More people were massacred. We never knew if we would survive the day. We just kept living and escaping as long as we could breathe. It was the only thing we could do.

During this time, I still had to look after my brother, Musa. Wherever he went, I went also. If he had to go to the stream to shower, I went with him. Even conjoined twins weren't this inseparable. Musa's frequent seizures made him an outcast among his peers. No one wanted to talk or play with him. They all thought he was possessed by some evil spirit and his seizures were scary to watch. A disease without a name! This was why everyone thought it best to avoid him. My mother and I were his 24–hour support system. We continued to care for him as we struggled to stay alive. But soon, I would have to make one of the hardest decisions in my young life.

While we were in one of the new villages we had fled to, we received very important news. It was good news, but we received it with mixed reactions. My sister, Abbigail, who was overseas in Australia, wanted us to go to the capital city, Freetown. She wanted us to stay there for a while, while she made arrangements for us to join her in Australia. I did not know Abbigail, for she had already gone overseas before I was born. An ex-soldier brought the news to us because at the time, not everyone could travel to and from the city except those who had trained and knew their way around different routes.

Indeed, Father had been correct with his advice to Abbigail. If he was alive, he could have reminded her of his words when he had said the destiny of the Bangura family was in her hands. However, what unfolded next had me search every part of my little mind for positive thoughts. It left me with a lifetime of pain.

The trip to Freetown was no joke. It was a very long journey from the village to the capital. But that was the least of our concerns. There was a civil war happening in the country, and rebel soldiers had barricaded every road, junction, and highway. To escape them, we would have to take the forests and uncharted roads. Even that was not entirely safe. Rebel soldiers still lurked in the bushes and deserted roads, and a woman with two young boys travelling together was sure to draw some attention.

Musa was also in very bad condition. His seizures had increased to more than five times a day. Each episode left him weaker than the last. How were we supposed to travel through rebel camps and past enemy soldiers undetected with my brother who could start thrashing around on the ground at any moment?

We thought and thought about it. There was nothing else we could do. Taking Musa along with us on this dreadful journey might mean death for all three of us. With just my mother and I...well, we could at least dream of making it to the other side. But with Musa, there was a 99.9% chance of failure. His body was also too weak to undertake such a long journey. We would have to spend days walking, from sunrise to sunset. Musa's body was already covered with wounds from the falls during his seizures and some of them were still fresh and had yet to heal. Musa would have to be left here. We would have to make the journey without him.

P-to-P opted to stay with him and when I broke down into tears, he promised that he and Musa would join us in the city when he was healed enough. That pacified me for a bit. But the thought of spending even a day without Musa broke me. It took coaxing and promises to get me to agree to my mother's decision.

An escort was sent to guide us to the city. He was an ex-soldier. At that time, there was no way of getting into the city but to walk for days. Only the rebels were allowed to drive vehicles. Any other vehicle that was seen on the road was stopped and set ablaze with its occupants inside. The other alternative was to travel by sea, using worn-out canoes and boats.

For the few days that followed, my mother secretly made preparations for our travel. Whatever little we had, she packed, including some food for the journey. At the same time, we continued to care for Musa as we had always done. Poor Musa...he did not suspect a thing, for neither my mother nor I had the heart to tell him that we would be leaving for the city to go overseas without him. Nor did we tell him that we may never see each other again. We snuck out of the house one Wednesday night when he was fast asleep.

It was raining so hard that night. I was beside myself with worry as my mother clutched my hand. We said goodbye to P-to-P as he locked the door behind us and hurried to our escort, who was patiently waiting on the corner for us.

As we hurried into the bushes, I turned to take one last longing look at the shadowy outline of our house as my mother pulled me along. My eyes were burning, and my heart felt heavy. I was almost 11 years old when we left home that day. I was still a child, but I already knew loss so deeply. I felt it as we walked further into the bushes, further from home and away from Musa.

But what could a boy who was barely 11 years old do? It wasn't as if I could cry and hold on to him. I knew my brother was very sick. But we had promised to stick close together. I knew nothing about how much danger we were about to step into by trying to leave the village. So, with all my innocence, I cried tears of guilt, desperately wishing my mother would let Musa come along. It would take me several years to finally heal from the trauma of the events that followed.

This was the last time I ever saw Musa, and my heart still aches to this day.

CHAPTER 9

Crossing Enemy Lines

The night provided a perfect cover for escape. Daytime was dangerous—anybody could be easily identified and shot. But in the darkness, there was a higher chance of safety—it was like hiding in plain sight. In addition to that, the rain helped to make sure that few people ventured outside, including the rebels. Everyone was too busy seeking shelter or trying to sleep in the cold weather. We were counting on that. As the rains poured heavily on us, we thanked the heavens for help. This seemed like a favourable situation, but it wasn't entirely so.

Heavy rains meant the bushes were more slippery and we were prone to flooded paths and creepy creatures that liked to be out when it rained. But even these hazards were the last thing on our minds. For what lay ahead could very well either be the beginning of new life for my mother and me, or the end of our already-miserable lives.

As we ventured further and further away from where I had called home all my life, I felt tears of fear in my eyes. I thought of the coming dawn and how Musa would wake to see an empty space where I used to lay.

He would go out, of course, to look for me. He would call my name in the fond way he used to address me. I imagined him asking P-to-P if he had seen me and P-to-P giving him an unclear answer.

Most of all, I worried about him having a seizure without me or Mother to look after him. Not even the rain poured more than my tears that night. My mother must have caught on to my pain for she drew me close and held me even tighter. In the silence, we exchanged some comfort in knowing that we were at least in this together. We had each other. In the most challenging times, you can choose to see things positively. The only thing I was able to do was wipe my tears.

I pulled in whatever was left of my tears. I had to be strong. At least for my mother. She had been through so much already and I did not want to have her worry too much about me. "Mama, let me carry our bags. I will carry them until we get to the city."

My mother's smile was warm as she turned to me. She knew better. "You cannot carry everything until we get to the city, my son," she responded. I was not going to let that deter me. I needed to be a man for my mother, so I insisted anyway. After six hours, I was already thoroughly exhausted. Being a man for mother would have to wait, I guess.

"You are my hero. I will help you now," were my mother's words of comfort to me after she noticed my tired shoulders slump with fatigue. We still had a very long way to go, and it had only begun to dawn on me now. Escaping was not going to be easy.

If I was still wondering how long we would have to walk, the next hours convinced me to give up such calculations. My mother and I continued to walk for another ten hours. Miles upon miles without any human in sight, except our escort ahead, and the sun had almost risen in the dark sky.

Drenched, soaked, and exhausted to the bone, we encountered our first sign of trouble. Up ahead of us was a river with a boat ashore. There was no one around to take us across. Our escort decided to investigate and went up into the water. When he returned, he delivered even scarier news. The canoe was in no condition to carry anyone across the river. It had holes in it and there were no oars to paddle across. To make matters worse, a strong wind was blowing, and the muddy, dark water rippled with waves that seemed to dare us to get in and perish.

We were stuck in the middle. We had already covered several miles and going back was never an option. At this point, neither was going forward. How do you take three people across a river in an oarless canoe filled with holes?

Time was not on our side, and our escort was very aware of that. "Do you trust me?" This was our escort's next question to my mother and me. Did we have a choice?

If we wanted to make it to the city alive, we had to rely on this man. So, even with our uncertainties, we followed his lead. Mother and I sat inside the canoe while he pushed the boat as fast as he could. Whatever law of physics he hoped to defy, I do not know.

However, necessity is the mother of invention. His desperation, and ours, was enough to get us partly into the river before the laws of nature caught up with us. What made things even worse was the fact that we did not know how to swim. It was uncommon to see anyone in my country back then who knew how to swim. It wasn't something that was taught.

When you go to a stream or a river, you just jump in and hope that somehow you would not drown. Whatever you could do to stay afloat, you did. That was it—that was our way of swimming. As we made our way across the river, water entered the canoe from the hole. And soon, the boat became too heavy to push.

We were sinking. In panic, we decided to throw out all our bags. Anything to lighten the boat. Throwing our bags out meant losing what little belongings and food we had stocked up. But what use was food to us anyway if we drowned?

We began by throwing the things we thought we needed less. Each throw helped lighten the boat. After a few minutes, it would begin to sink again, and that meant we had to throw out more. As we paddled across, our loads and bags reduced. By the time we made it to the other end of the shore, there was nothing left to throw. Everything had to go. It was either that or our lives. We eventually made it across to the other shore with only our lives to spare. We barely survived.

Our clothes were already worn and drenched from the storm, and struggling to push a leaking boat had certainly not helped our case at all. At this point, one would think that perhaps we should take a break. My feet were injured and sore. I was not sure how much longer I could stand on them. But we couldn't even stop for a moment. Rest was only an option if we wanted to die.

Daylight had almost arrived and as the sun rose, our chances of survival got slimmer.

The bushes again were the safest option. We could not take the village paths.

So, like animals, we scurried through the jungle, ducking at the slightest noise we heard. It had rained the night before, so the earth and grass were still moist. The air was cold and smelled of plants and wet soil. It had a smell that was both musky, yet fresh. The kind that made you want to inhale deeply. But we were not afforded the luxury of pausing to appreciate the beauty of the nature around us. If anything, this nature could very well be our dying place if we were not careful enough. We walked as briskly as we could, treading through moist grass, careful not to let our feet make too much noise. On several occasions, the bushes would cause us to slip as they were moist and slimy. And as for the heavy branches above us, they would intermittently drip leftover water over our heads as we took cover under them. After the rains, the animals came out to play too, so we had to constantly watch where we were going to avoid stepping on poisonous crawling reptiles and other creeping creatures.

Whenever we reached an open path, my mother and I had to hide in the bushes while our escort scanned the area for any signs of rebels or their gangs.

One slight mistake from him could very well cost us our lives and his. Aiding us to escape was already a crime punishable by execution at the hands of those savage rebels. Waiting in hiding while our escort went to scan the open areas was both nerve-wracking and excruciating. Sometimes, he would be gone for hours. Rebels liked to hide too, so he had an entire expanse of land, measuring into several acres, to scan before he could declare it safe for us to cross.

Often, when he took a bit too long to return, my mother and I would spend hours waiting silently, unsure if he would ever return to us and wondering if he had been captured. My mother would then give me a look that said, *It's just you and me now if he does not return.*

We always had the same questions on our mind. *How long would we wait? Should we continue to hide or try to go further by ourselves?* Questions upon questions, a never-ending cycle of doubt and fear.

And as the waiting turned into hours, I could see fear begin to creep into my mother's eyes. Tears came out silently. We were too afraid to even sob. And each time, as I turned to look into her eyes, I could sense her anxiety. Her tear-filled eyes broke my little heart even more. I would give anything to see her smile again. Would she ever? Would we even make it out alive?

When we were not busy comforting each other, I would sit still with my mother beside me and stare up at the bluish-white sky. The colour of the sky remained the same regardless of what was happening around us. It was still beautiful and magnificent. I often wondered how high up the sky really was, yet I could never fully fathom it. Why was the sky blue? How did the whitish foam, which I now know are clouds, come about? And did the rains fall from the sky or from our roofs?

Thankfully, our escort returned every time, eventually. I have no idea how long my mother and I would have lasted without him or what we would have done.

After several days of hunger, thirst, and fighting for survival every second, my mother did something surprising. She looked up into the sky and counted, "Five, four, three, two, one." Then, she said, "Today is your birthday, son."

I turned 11 that day. Just 11 years of life, yet I had been through so much already. To survive, I had to learn to act more like an adult than a child. In fact, I can barely recall having a normal childhood or even being dependent as a child should be. I cared for my sick brother, hid from rebel attacks in our village, and undertook a life-or-death journey. It sure had been an eventful 11 years of my life. But there was more to come.

By this point, my feet, hands, and every part of my body was starting to give up on me. I could no longer walk. My feet were sore, and I was so hungry I thought I was going to pass out. Our escort saw the state I was in and finally allowed us to stop for a rest in one village. Before we could even do this, he had to scan the entrance to the village and the path to be sure it was safe for us. Again, the bushes, our friend, provided the cover we needed while we waited for our escort to return.

An hour later, our escort was still nowhere to be seen. My mother and I were hiding silently in the forest next to the village. It was almost dark. The sun was setting lazily over the horizon—a pale-orange colour spread across the sky. Dusk was here, and we had been in hiding for hours. As usual, I kept looking at my mother's face to get a sense of how bad things really were. This time, every emotion was etched so clearly on her face. Her shiny, brown eyes glistened with fresh tears. We huddled together and it got so hot having to share such a small space together for so long. I longed to comfort her in some way. So, I gave it a shot.

Holding her pinkie, I whispered, "Everything is going to be okay. God is in control, remember?" Those were my mother's favourite words when things went haywire. I figured at least hearing them from me would give her some sort of comfort, and it did. Upon hearing me, my mother quickly pulled herself together and reassured me with a tiny smile that stretched across the expanse of her stressed and fatigued face.

For the first time in several hours, I saw my mother smile. I immediately jumped to my feet and tried out a few stretches. Her smile had infused me with strength again and I felt hopeful. Almost in sync with this new air of hope, our escort returned. He brought back news. We could go into the village at last.

Tired and hungry, we had barely found shelter in the village when I noticed that my feet were swelling. Hours of trekking had taken a toll on my young legs. Mother's solution was simple. I would place my feet in a bucket of warm salt water. Her solution worked and soon, the painful aches began to subside. Throughout the night, my mother and our escort did not sleep. They were busy brainstorming ideas for our journey the next day. This was the most dangerous part of our journey.

You see, at this point, the only way forward was to go through the rebels' camp. Once we got through the rebels' camp, there was only one last river to cross. There was no alternative. This was the only route we had left. The one thing that stood between us and the river were the rebel soldiers who had somehow managed to set up a checkpoint on that same path.

Just before the blessed oblivion of sleep caressed my tender eyes, I stared at my mother. I heard the fear in her voice as she and our escort spoke in hushed tones. Was tonight our last night? I inched close to my mother and clutched her very tightly. If we did not make it out alive tomorrow, at least I had tonight.

Morning came quickly. It was similar to waking up in our village. There was the familiar crow of the roosters, and mothers calling out to their children. There was also the sound of fathers preparing to hunt or farm. The only thing that was different was the look of dread and gloom on everyone's face. The war had changed everything and everyone. Children no longer roamed the compounds playing, nor did women gather to share stories and laugh. Everyone was solemn, almost waiting for something bad to happen. The scars of war...it felt as though everyone had these inflicted upon them.

My feet were still sore, but not as sore as my heart. If we wanted any shot at survival, we had to keep moving. After a few hours, we decided to take shelter under a large tree while our escort resumed his job of scouting the path ahead of us. The more we trekked, the more reality dawned on us. We were getting closer and closer to the rebels' camp. What would we do?

How would we escape the watchful, hawk-like eyes of the rebel soldiers? What was the plan?

Well, my mother and our escort managed to come up with something. It was very risky, but it was either that or nothing. We had to go undercover. We were going to pretend to be part of the rebel battalion. If anyone asked, we were members of the rebel camp.

It was a 50/50 chance of survival. We would either cross through the camp successfully without being detected or be exposed and face detention or death. We could be killed if they found out we were not real members of the rebel camp.

Just before we began this emotional and tense journey into enemy lines, my mother pulled me aside. "If anything is to happen to me, you must always be kind to people and try, by all means, to get to safety. And if possible, make it to Freetown."

I stared at her, unable to say a word. My mother was saying her final goodbyes to me. It was almost like that time when Samba had talked to us just before running into the burning house that had eventually buried him. My mother was the only parent I had left. I had watched one parent die and now another was bidding me goodbye.

Even though I was a child, I felt a sense of dread and heaviness in my chest. I already knew what it meant to feel loss. And in that moment, as my mother and I said what could very well be our last prayers, my heart began to race. In my small rib cage, my heart thudded so loudly that I feared my mother would hear it. Our escort returned with word. It was time to leave.

We walked towards the rebel camp in the direction of the river where our fate awaited us. I remember promising myself that I would survive no matter what.

I had to. I did not leave Musa and everyone else behind to come this far and die. I had to survive. How I would do that was another matter entirely.

I was so lost in thought that I did not realise we were getting close to the river. A sudden heavy downpour began. We didn't want to take shelter in any of the village huts for fear of the rebels, so we continued our journey. What was a heavy downpour compared to losing our lives? We would rather be drenched.

As we passed some of the cabins, we could clearly see some of the rebels taking refuge from the rain. Some of them carried big guns while the others had weapons in their hands. Everyone gazed at us briefly as we walked past, and for a moment, we felt safe. None of them bothered to question us.

But that did not continue for long. Soon, the brief gazes turned to stares and the stares turned into suspicious whispers. Our escort sensed it too, and signalled for us to stop. He quickly pulled us aside and decided to outsmart the rebels.

Taking a piece of rope, he tied my mother's hands and mine together. The plan was to make us look like his captives as we were already attracting too much suspicion. Our escort's quick thinking is probably the only reason I'm alive today to tell this story, for when we approached the last rebel camp leading to the river, we heard an angry voice command us to halt.

"STOP! What the hell are you guys doing here?" he yelled.

My mother and I turned at the same time. A boy not much older than me was responsible for yelling the command to stop. Our escort quickly bowed to him.

My eyes widened with shock. This ... This boy was their commander?

"I captured them," our escort replied. "They are my captives who I am taking across the river to kill in front of our other family members for disrespecting me."

The boy along with his comrades immediately burst into laughter. They took their guns and poked my mother and me, while stuttering with laughter. As they mocked us, my mother and I trembled with fear. We were about to lose our lives and these men were having the best time of theirs.

When they were done, one of the rebels told our escort that they would help him end our miserable lives. "We can do it now," he added before another round of laughter erupted among the group. My mother and I trembled even more. We were soaked and hungry, and the way they joked about our lives convinced us how fickle our survival truly was.

Our escort was quick to respond. "No, I want to do it in front of our family to serve as a warning to others."

The boy whispered something into his comrade's ear and his comrade then walked inside the barracks. When he returned, he handed an axe and a long machete to the boy. Staring at me straight in the eye, the boy asked me, "Long hand or shorthand?"

I had no clue what he meant so I stood there, silent and shivering. For one thing, he did not look old or scary and could have easily been an elder brother to me. What could this strange question mean? Did he want to play a game with me? All these questions floated around in my mind as the boy continued his staring match with me.

I only realised something was wrong when I heard my mother sob and saw her fall to the ground. This boy was not playing any game with me, I realised a tad late. My mother was crying and begging for the boy to take her instead.

"Ma mu, tae mbk ma tar more, ma mu papa!" she kept begging in our native language. When translated, it means, "Do not cut off his hands, please. He would be useless without them!"

Then it dawned on me. I was going to lose my

hands! And in the most casual of ways. He had simply asked me which tool I preferred. Whichever one I chose would determine how much of my arm he would chop off. I then realised why he was their commander. He was not someone who could have easily been my elder brother, as I had naively thought.

If my heart had been racing before, this time it threatened to fly out of my chest.

It was still raining, but hot sweat broke out from my forehead. My face was flushed, and my mouth was dry. Adrenaline was coursing through my arms and legs, and I was ready to run.

How far would I get before I dropped dead? These boys had guns. Still, I'd rather be dead than stand alive and watch them chop off my arms.

My mother was still on the wet ground sobbing, begging for them to spare me and take her instead. I dropped to my knees too and joined the begging party. I was desperately begging a boy not more than 18 years old to spare my life.

As we knelt, the rain poured harder, flooding the

area. We were knee-deep in the sand, tears pouring uncontrollably. My mother wailed. She begged to be the sacrificial lamb, while I, at 11 years old, was about to have my arms chopped off.

After what seemed like an eternity, the commander looked at us and told our escort that we could go, but there was one condition. Our escort had to return with proof and stories of how he killed us. With relief, our escort agreed and pulled us to the riverbank where other rebels and captured civilians were lined up waiting for the boat.

Our escort signalled for us to keep our hands tied. We were not completely safe until we reached Freetown.

Barely recovered from my close call with death, I stumbled onto the boat, half dead from fear. My mother continued to sniff and sob silently. The boat was overloaded with both humans and luggage, but no one seemed to care. There were no safety jackets, and it was likely most of the people on the boat didn't know how to swim. What if we capsized? How would this small vessel be able to make it across the stormy waves with this many people on board? Nobody had a bloody clue! As I relayed my fears to my mother, she gave me the same expression she'd had just before Samba had entered the burning building.

"Everything will be okay, my son," she tried comforting me even though I could see the terror in her eyes. Leaning into her for comfort, I held onto her as the boat towed on. As the boat pulled away from the bank, I felt my mother sigh with relief. We made it on the boat. Finally!

We finally made it after days of trekking through forests, hiding from rebels, and eating nothing but fruits. Even after all those dangers we faced, we finally made it! I could barely hold back my tears.

I had almost lost my arms only minutes before, yet here I was. I was a survivor.

Something inside me was burning with determination. I made it this far.

I survived a war that had cost me so much and was now on my way to Freetown, 'The city of light', as my mother used to call it.

I was indeed a survivor! And survive I would. I would not die.

It was with this conviction that I looked towards the horizon, while leaning on the woman who held my hand and guided me onward—my mother.

If anything, I had to live for her. We did not come this far to lose!

CHAPTER 10

Freetown—But We Weren't Free

Being in the city for the very first time was amazing. As soon as we arrived in Freetown, our saviour, the escort, disappeared. I was too busy staring and pointing at the tall buildings, cars, and people to even notice when he left. I never got to thank the man who put his life on the line, time and time again, for us on this journey.

It was getting dark when we arrived at 5th Street. I remember staring, wide-eyed and mouth agape, as we passed several houses and apartment buildings. *How could there be so many buildings?* I thought. *Was there even enough space for humans?*

And cars. There were a lot of them. The fanciest vehicle I had ever seen in my life had been the village Poda Poda, which often brought people from the city. Now, if the Poda Poda caught my fancy, you can only imagine how amazed I was when I saw even shinier cars!

To my fascinated, boyish eyes, the city was heaven to me compared to all I had ever known back in the village. I could not understand how there were so many people. Even the air smelled different. Everywhere I looked seemed bare, and I only saw a few small trees and bushes. The grass was gone; it was replaced with black floors, which they called roads. I was impressed. Everything tickled my fancy.

As we made our way through the city, I stopped and stared constantly at the things around me, and my mother had to keep pulling me forward. My mouth hung open and my eyes almost popped out of their sockets. My optimistic spirit surprised my mother. She could not believe my reaction. Even though I had witnessed the gruesome effects of the war, I was still able to appreciate this new place. She called me her little hero and praised my high spirits.

In 2000, Sheik and Hass had managed to go overseas. Even though everyone seemed to be going about their business without any care, there was still suspicion and fear in their hearts. Whenever there was a loud noise, an eerie silence followed, and many people would run and hide. These false triggers were proof that even though the war seemed like it was coming to an end, it was far from over within us.

One popular activity among those of us who successfully moved to Freetown was reminiscing and sharing horrid details of our survival experiences. It was almost like a competition—trying to see who had the most terrible experience to tell. Everyone looked forward to these times, for there was always a feeling of comradeship among us as we shared our stories. It was like a reassurance that we weren't alone.

One night, not long after we arrived, I exhibited my first sign of PTSD. As to be expected, none of us had a clue that it was something we should have taken more seriously.

That night, it was story time as usual. An elderly lady, who was one of the occupants in the apartment we now called our home, decided to share her own survival story.

She called it the Judgement Day that happened on January 6th, 1999. This was the day that changed our nation forever. From her experience, she narrated how pandemonium had broken out, and shared how parents abandoned their kids and vice versa. Families were torn apart, and husbands watched their wives get raped by the rebels. Children and women were forced to watch family members burn in a building while the rebels stood guard to shoot whoever attempted to escape the flames.

The elderly lady recalled hiding in a house with a pregnant woman when the rebels stormed through the building and came into their apartment. They brought out the pregnant woman and asked her for the sex of her child. When the lady tearfully replied that she did not know, they began to debate how they would have to find out if the child was a boy or a girl. In the end, they concluded that they would have to cut out the baby from the mother to confirm the child's gender.

At this point, my imaginative mind was clearly painting each scene as she described them. Like a flash of light, suddenly, I could see Samba. I was back at the scene where he had rushed into the burning building. I could see him yelling and screaming in pain as the flames engulfed him.

I did not even realise that I had stood up and began to run. I was running and screaming while calling Samba's name. My mother immediately stood and ran after me. When she finally grabbed me, she patted me softly on the back.

"Hushhh, it's okay now. Samba died a hero."

Slowly, I calmed down and collapsed into her arms, barely able to catch my breath. I was only 12 years old.

From time to time, my mother and I would talk about Musa and how hard things must be for him back at the village. Our greatest fear was how he was coping without us to support him. On some nights, I would wake up screaming from nightmares I had of him calling out to me and begging me to help him. I would wake up in tears, sweating intensely and out of breath. After each nightmare, I would tearfully pray to God and ask him to keep my brother safe.

One morning, my mother called me over. She had news. I would return to school.

I knew we could not afford it, so I asked her how that was possible.

"I have spoken to one of our family friends and she has agreed to take you in as an errand boy," she told me.

I would be working as 'house help', as it was more commonly named. In exchange for doing home chores for this family friend, they would assist in paying for my school fees and upkeep.

I was not in full support of my mother's new plan. I had grown accustomed to being with her. Now, barely even a year into living in Freetown, we were going to be apart. With huge reluctance and doubts, I finally agreed. I thought perhaps she knew something I didn't know yet.

Weeks passed and it was time for me to leave for my new job. With worries and great sorrow, my mother and I packed what little belongings I had left. All I had were two pairs of shorts, a round-neck, black shirt, and a grey-and-white striped, old, dirty dress shirt. What I managed to survive the war with, I took with me.

My mother got me ready for my new job by shaving off my hair. It was looking too bushy and unkempt, according to her. She did not just trim off the overgrown hair, she removed all of it!

And even to this day, my mother only approves of my hairstyle if I shave everything off. To her, that is the perfect definition of a clean cut. Anything else is no good in her books.

With a heavy heart, I finally bade my mother goodbye and began my journey to the other end of the city, where our family friend's house was located. Once I arrived, I thought it definitely had to be heaven. I had never seen a house so big and so beautiful. The family friend (who I began to call Aunty) and other house occupants were all incredibly lovely and showed me my sleeping quarters. Before that day, I'd never had a bed or slept in one. I had always slept on the floor.

With awe and excitement, I began to explore this castle! I familiarised myself with the new surroundings and quickly learned new things. I was also introduced to my niece, who was about the same age as I was.

Those were some of my best days! There was so much to eat, plenty to drink, and lots of time to rest. Life couldn't have been any better. After a few days, Aunty gifted me my school uniform—the first I had ever worn. I remember holding the uniform solemnly. I felt a rush of different emotions as I stared at what would become mine. I was to resume school the next day.

I could vividly recall how school had been for me back in Madina. We sat on the bare floor with our bottoms on the ground. The ground wasn't some clean floor; it was red soil mixed with dirt, but we did not mind. It was the norm. We sat and wrote on the dusty ground. Sometimes, when we were sure the teacher wasn't looking, we played with it, too. So, it made learning all the more fun. Getting to play with sand was every child's favourite thing to do. At the end of the school day, we would head home with our bottoms dirty and dusty, and our palms and fingernails filled with red soil.

But it wasn't that way in this place. We didn't have to sit on the ground. There were chairs and desks. And instead of the dust, we wrote on books with pencils and pens. What a stark contrast to the life I had known!

The night before my first day of school, sleep fled from me. I had so many thoughts and worries. What would going to school for the first time be like? Was it too late for me to start school? Would I be able to stay seated in one place for the whole day?

By morning, however, I was early to rise. Even though I was confused and anxious, I was also excited to start this new chapter of my life. When I arrived at school, the swarm of faces greatly worried me. There were so many children with different faces. It looked like the perfect place to get lost. The school building itself was half finished, but I did not mind. It felt so overwhelming to be in this environment and instantly, I resolved to make sure I worked hard. I don't know why it happens, but it just does. Whenever I feel overwhelmed or challenged by a situation, my first thoughts are about how to overcome it. Maybe it was one of the gifts that surviving the war gave me.

As time went on, I grew accustomed to being referred to as the 'house help'. I had lived in the house of my family friend for 12 months now. For those months, I had been treated like a prince, or a couple on their honeymoon days. Those days of bliss, with enough food to eat and even time to rest, began to dwindle as I continued to live with them. It was like they were welcoming me to reality, and I had been living in a mirage all this while.

But after the first year, there were far more chores to do and less time to rest. Whenever I failed to complete a task, I would be whipped as a punishment and sometimes given less food. I was very grateful for my aunt's support in my education, but since I had just started, I had a lot to catch up on. I was already behind on time and needed to study harder than my mates. How could I study when there was no time at all for me? I dared not say a word though, so I continued on this path until my grades too began to suffer.

I knew what I had to do. I had to visit my mother. If there was anyone in the world who would understand me, it was my mother. And so, I paid her a visit and voiced all my concerns. She knew it was hard for me, but we were scared. Without money and adequate space in my mother's place, returning home was not advisable. Besides, what would happen to my education? It was very difficult to even gather enough to eat. What would we do?

In the end, I decided to endure the situation and hope that change would come. After several months without any improvement, I opted to return to my mother's house. Months later, my sisters Baida, Salamatu, and my mother found the courage and finances to bring them and their children to live with us in our house. The whereabouts of both Baida's and Salamatu's husbands were unknown.

I have watched my sister Salamatu battle

numerous illnesses. Her courage is what I continue to admire most about her. Even though she was plagued with sickness and often sent for treatment to various native doctors, she would always return with a smile and new strength for life. I often ask myself how she does it. Finally, I asked her one day. "Sister, how do you manage being sick all the time?"

She looked down at me with her strong, beautiful eyes—eyes that penetrated my soul—and said, "Brother, we make use of what we have." With that, she embraced me, and we held on to each other. Neither of us wanted to break that moment. Her embrace was warm, and she felt like home. Home before the war, before the separation, before the deaths. The young me held on to her because that was all I could do.

We would find a way to get by—I was sure.

But things were even more tough. My mother had to work as a maid in other people's houses to support my schooling and all of us. We did not have much. In fact, we were barely surviving, but we were content and grateful for the little we had. If anything, we knew it could've been worse.

At night, after the daily hustle, we would all gather in a circle to share our experiences for the day. We laughed with glee as if we had no care in the world.

These warm moments are some of the things I am most grateful for, and they helped make the tough times more bearable.

In 2002, the brutal civil war ended. Some of my siblings managed to go overseas. Some lived in different parts of Freetown, but we were not all aware of each other's whereabouts. Our family was very large, so it was hard to keep track of everybody. There were so many siblings who I hadn't seen since I was born.

We later learnt that Salamatu's husband, due to his advanced educational status, was privileged to travel overseas to study. He later sent for my sister and their children. I remember when the news carrier arrived and told her the news that she was travelling overseas. She cried from joy as she went around hugging her family members, including myself. She whispered to me that I needed to ensure I kept tabs on her eldest daughter, Shishi, who was adopted at birth by our deceased uncle's wife, Barbay. I promised my sister I would be her shadow. A few days later, my sister left to an unknown land to meet her husband.

By this time, I was 14 years old and back at school. I continued to work extra hard and even got a double promotion to skip two grades ahead. Things were going well with us and seemed to get even better when we got news from my elder sister, Abigail. She wanted us to go to Conakry, Guinea, for a humanitarian program to enable us to travel to Australia. This was the very news we had been waiting so long for. It began to feel like everything was working out well after all.

At school, I met my friend, Isha, who later turned out to be my first crush. Even though I was a teenage boy, I still fondly remember thinking she was the most beautiful girl I had ever seen in my life. I remember telling my best friend at the time that when I was old enough, I would marry Isha. He just laughed at me and called my dreams mere talk. Isha and I became fast friends. She was a very kind soul.

Sometimes, she would give me money or bring lunch for me when things became tough at home. We spent time with each other daily. She was the love of my teenage life. There was no technology then, so we devised a way to meet up at night. I would sneak into her backyard and throw a small rock at their rooftop. It was our signal. She would come out to meet me once she heard the sound.

That seemed to work for us for a while, until we ran out of luck. I snuck around one night, like I always did, and threw a rock. This time, her elder sister came out and chased me away. Apparently, we had been caught. She abused me while threatening to report the matter to my mother. Well, that did not bother Isha and me at all. We simply had to limit when we saw each other. We only saw each other during the day on our trek to school, during school hours, and our trek back home from school.

As I tried to navigate fitting into the school environment and puberty, I began to establish several friendships along the way. One particular friend stood out from the rest: my best friend, who I nicknamed 'Shaggy'.

Shaggy and I were always together. We were

practically inseparable. The only time we were apart from each other was at night when we went to bed. Our closeness was so strong that people began to mistake us for brothers. Like Siamese twins, we were so connected and shared a deep bond with each other. Shaggy and I were the youngest members of our local religious committee. We went to meetings, prayers, and fundraising events together. We even joined the local soccer club together where we trained twice a week and played a tournament every Saturday. For a very long time, we did everything together.

One fateful day, I woke up bright and cheerful like I always did whenever Shaggy and I had plans to hang out. I remember hurrying out of bed with happiness flashing through me like a comet. As soon as I was done freshening up, I skipped along for a few blocks to Shaggy's house. With my right hand in my pocket, a plastered grin on my face, and anticipation in my heart, I knocked on the bright-yellow door that stood in front of the porch of his house.

One, two, three, and then several more knocks. Nobody responded. I continued hammering the door, but each time, only the silence of the morning echoed back. My knuckles almost stung with pain as the smile on my face began to evaporate like steam. Finally, one of the neighbours looked through the window and passed on the news that shattered me completely. "Shaggy does not live there anymore."

That was it. Nothing else. I stared in disbelief. "What do you mean he does not live here anymore?" I asked with fear creeping into my entire body. I was with Shaggy just the day before.

"He left with his family last night," the neighbour continued before leaving me to my fate.

The sky immediately changed from blue to grey. The tears began to rain down as I buried my face in my hands. I was beyond devastated. How could Shaggy be gone? How could he leave without saying goodbye? I had so many questions.

Above all, I was broken that the one person I had come to completely trust and love so much since coming to Freetown was gone, and I had no idea where he went. I walked home, face down with my hands on my head. I headed straight into the small, dark living room to sulk on the palm tree leaf chair. I refused to go outside. I was lonely and depressed. There was no way I was socialising with anyone.

For the next weeks that followed, everyone, including my mother, tried to cheer me up, but nothing worked. With Shaggy gone, all I was left with was a deep sense of emptiness. After two weeks, he finally called from a neighbour's phone and explained that he was now in America. He said he didn't tell me he was leaving because his parents gave him strict instructions not to say anything until he arrived in America.

Hearing from him helped me heal faster. At least I now knew that I was in no way at fault and that there was nothing I could have done to keep Shaggy from leaving. Shaggy's leaving caused me to withdraw from people.

Weeks and months passed before I started to come out of my shell again. I began to interact with others and make new friends, but I never got too close to anyone for fear of losing someone again. It was a real case of once bitten, twice shy.

Life continued without any noteworthy events

until we received news that my sister, Baida, her daughter, Mariama, and my mother and I were to travel to the neighbouring country, Guinea, to start the process of migrating to Australia.

Since we received the information as urgent news via a neighbour's phone, we had to leave quickly without further ado. My mother and Baida rallied around, preparing what they could as time was hardly on our side. It was during these preparations that we received one of the saddest pieces of news that we have ever experienced. On the very day we were supposed to leave Freetown, a messenger brought word that my beloved brother Musa had just died in the village.

All the excitement of leaving Freetown to go to another country quickly vanished. My mother, Baida, and I immediately began to weep and mourn. My heart felt as if it were being squeezed. I felt as though I was standing alone in a dark place without any help. Words will never be able to describe the emotions I felt after I heard the news about Musa. He was the closest to me of all my brothers. I had come to know the world with Musa by my side and had never completely forgiven myself for leaving him behind, even though it was clearly beyond my control.

My mother felt as much pain as I did. He was her son, after all. As I watched my mother cry uncontrollably, my heart ached more. I did not even get to say goodbye.

At this point, we had a very difficult decision to make. It was either we went back to the village for the funeral, to pay our respects to our own blood, or continue our travel plans to a new country. If we went back, we would lose the opportunity to start a new life in a new country and our dreams of migration might be indefinitely cancelled. If we did not go back, we would not be able to give Musa his last rites as well as pay respects to his soul. It would be as though we had abandoned him both in life and in death.

Throughout that day, my mother and everyone sat with a sense of disorientation. We were both heartbroken and confused. What would we do? In our despair, we remembered how my biological father and Samba had passed away and the several losses the family had endured, including those we did not have the chance to mourn properly. We certainly did not deserve to experience all these misfortunes, but what could we do?

By 11 pm, we made a decision. We would continue the journey. That night, we would continue with our travel plans to Guinea. That would mean that we would not be able to properly mourn Musa, nor would we be able to pay him the final rites he deserved. Gathering ourselves together, we prayed for his soul and went ahead with the plan.

CHAPTER 11

Answered Prayers

With our hearts still heavy and our eyes swollen from hours of crying, we began another sad, long journey. We had no public transport and certainly no vehicle of our own except our legs—if you could count that. We walked and walked for about seven miles to the ferry terminal as it was the only means of transportation available for us. Having been delayed a bit due to the news of Musa's passing, we were worried that we wouldn't be able to catch a ferry.

However, we were lucky enough to get the last ferry going to Kasseri, which is the border shared by Sierra Leone and Guinea. Sitting by the ferry window, I stared outside watching the starlit sky. I wondered what the future held for me and my loved ones. I cannot recall how long I stared, but slowly, the night sky began to subside, and a beautiful sun began to rise.

Suddenly, it struck me. I had a purpose. I whispered to the universe that I was meant to survive and tell the world the story of the family with 24 children. This was the reason I somehow kept surviving all these ordeals—the vision was getting clearer. My mother's voice snapped me out of my trance.

We had finally arrived in Guinea.

Looking around, I discovered there was not much difference between Guinea and my hometown. However, they were living in peace and the aftermath of the war that we had been living with was noticeably absent. Eager to begin our new life, we headed over to the quarters that had been arranged for us. The complexity of the people we would be living with made us feel alienated at first. They spoke a completely different language and had values that were different from ours. We were total strangers in the community.

The complex we rented had four houses with three families occupying each house. As time went on, we began to learn about their culture and language and started to socialize with them. I even became friends with the girls who were around the same age as me in the complex: Jennaba, Yasmeen, Mariam, Hawanatu, and Kadiatu.

These girls were always in my room and sometimes even fought about who would get to sit next to me. This eventually became a source of worry for my mother.

My mother eventually insisted that they left after a certain time in the evening.

"If any of these girls fall pregnant, we would be in big trouble and that would jeopardise our journey," my mother often said to me.

However, I had no sexual experience at that time. I was simply a naïve virgin who enjoyed the female attention. Those girls grew to become like family to me and were a huge help with our integration into the community. They offered a lot of help to my mother and myself. When we had to go to the market, they would tag along to help us negotiate the prices of foods and other goods. On Sunday, all shops and markets were closed so everyone could relax and engage in sports. Every Sunday, Jennaba and Yasmeen would take me to each of these games. They were like my female bodyguards.

In time, my teenage attractions led me to a girl named Rama, who lived in the next complex. Rama spoke French, Soso. and Fullah, while I spoke Kerio and English, so understanding each other was a big challenge. Jennaba and Yasmeen were already picking up a few words in Kerio. Kerio is broken English. This meant that there were several words in Kerio that were pronounced the same in plain English. But for someone who had never heard it spoken before, they only understood a few words. It was at this point that I needed Jennaba and Yasmeen the most.

When Rama was around, they had to interpret Kerio to her and then translate her responses to me. Most times, we would be content with looking at each other and exchanging smiles.

We seemed to be integrating into the community reasonably well and were even recognised and liked by a few indigenes as well. However, I was about to be the centre of a storm that would rock our peaceful boat.

It was a Friday afternoon and the whole community seemed to be in a festive spirit. Everyone looked merry, as if there was a celebration to be had. On closer observation, I could see several people wearing their country's soccer team jerseys. It was then I realised there was a soccer match happening. It was Guinea's national soccer team against Tunisia in North Africa.

Back in Freetown, we were free to support whatever team we wanted. But in Guinea, things were different, and I had not the slightest clue!

I made the biggest mistake. After considering each team's strengths and seeing that the odds were in favour of Tunisia, I publicly declared that I would be supporting Tunisia. At 7 pm, the entire suburb, consisting of boys and girls—young and old—went to the only house in the area that had a television. Imagine a whole suburb going to watch TV in one house. Now, imagine the TV in a less-than-average room size of 3.2m x 3m.

The television was a thick, big box with two bulky nubs on the side that were used to manually change the channels. I came to realise as an adult that the size of the television would have been no larger than 15 inches.

I stood amongst the crowd like a drop of water in a lake. People used their knees to push me from the back and poked my head with their hands. I didn't realise that the people around me were acting in a completely different way. This is simply because I was supporting another team. By 9 pm, the game ended and so did my fate. Guinea lost!

In the morning, no one talked to me or responded to my greetings. I was perplexed. I was the complex's favourite new kid. Why was I getting the silent treatment? I would soon find out.

Right before lunch, the adults came to have a talk with my mother. We could no longer stay at the complex. We would need to find new accommodation. Just like that, our friendly neighbours and friends turned hostile. I lost my bodyguards, friends, and interpreters. This was the consequence of a random action. If only I had known. I tried to apologise, stating that it was not deliberate and that I had no idea I was not allowed to support other teams. In the end, it was decided. We would leave the complex.

Imagine losing your home because you supported a different team! Funny, right?

But it wasn't.

At least not for our family, who had to struggle to find shelter all over again. We eventually found another accommodation. It was located a few streets from our former complex. This time, we lived as quietly as we could, while waiting for the one call that would determine our future. These hard times made me appreciate Mama Salon. There, I had the choice to support the team I wanted to support.

Just as we were approaching the first-year anniversary of our arrival in Guinea, heaven finally smiled on us. We got the call for our first interview.

Imagine that you apply for a job and put in your application. The company calls you for an interview to ask follow-up questions and to check to make sure the application aligns with the applicant. In a similar manner, when Abbigail submitted our application for the humanitarian visa, the Australia government sent a representative to interview us to ensure our story aligned with the application. As a child, I just thought these people wanted to hear some of the trouble, and sometimes funny stories of the war. I had plenty stories.

I could not believe it. Neither did my family.

Finally, we had been given a shot at this golden opportunity. We were finally migrating to a white man's land.

What do you do if you are in the situation where making one mistake could very well cost—not just you, but the entire family—an opportunity of a better future? How would you feel?

This was the tight spot my mother was in. Just before we went into the interview room, she became tense and began to feel very sick. The pressure had gotten to her, and her body was giving up. It was so serious that the interview had to be postponed for a few hours.

After some hours of hugging and comforting her, we assured ourselves that my mother would do well. We tried to uplift her by being optimistic and not showing our own nervousness. We knew the gravity of the situation we were in. This was our last resort and hope. We had sacrificed so much just for this. We could not afford to lose. Unfortunately, the power to win was not entirely in our hands.

As soon as my mother regained her composure, we made a second attempt. Rallying behind her like chicks to a mother hen, we entered the imposing office of the white man who would determine our fate. This was my very first encounter with a white man and I was visibly in awe.

Of course, he was human and had the same parts we had; the only difference was that he seemed very fair, or white, as we often called them. Still, I was impressed and delighted to be in his presence. He had a majestic air around him that commanded respect and I was all too eager to tell my friends that I had met a white man. Not just met him, but he also shook my hand and spoke to me. I could not wait to see their eyes light up with both surprise and disbelief.

My mother sat in front while Baida, Baida's daughter, and I all sat slightly behind her. And then, the interview began. The first question was about the life we lived back at home. Slowly, we began to relive the horrors of the war with the help of an interpreter. We relayed everything we had encountered during the civil war. Everything from the deaths we had witnessed to our near-death experiences, and things we had to do to survive the rebel attacks. The scars were still fresh, so we recounted them with the clarity and the tenacity with which we experienced them.

The man seemed drawn in by our stories and asked several questions in a bid to get more information and understand our situation. We had to explain why we should be given the opportunity to travel abroad. My mother had to recount our life story to this stranger, and he appeared to be quite attentive as he watched my mother explain.

Just as she reached the part about the house collapsing with Samba inside, her hands and lips began to shake as the memory evoked heart-breaking emotions. Soon, she began to sob very loudly. She shed deep, gut-wrenching tears that would break anyone who listened.

By the end of the interview, her eyes were red, and her face was pale. As for the rest of us, we were nervous wrecks because we knew what would happen if we failed this interview. Our lives and future gravely depended on it.

We were directed to the waiting room and were asked to wait for the outcome. We sat together in silence, holding hands and praying. We did not have to wait for long.

30 minutes later, the door that held an answer that we prayed would be favourable opened. The interpreter was here with news.

We tried to read his expressions and searched his face for any clues. We hated the suspense he brought, and my mother began to sob quietly again. A few of us could barely stand with the anxiety quivering our legs.

The moment we had been fighting for had finally come and we were not prepared for how it felt. Looking at each of us one after the other, the interpreter finally spoke.

"I'm-I'm sorry for all you have gone through. But congratulations!"

Everyone gave a huge sigh of relief, and some of us even gave a loud cheer with a fist bump. We gathered for a group hug, and we couldn't help but cry. This time though, they were happy tears. Our prayers had been answered. We could not contain our excitement. All our struggles had not been in vain. We had not come this far for nothing.

With the successful interview, we had now qualified to progress into the next stage: our medical examination. The entire process up until the final award of our travel visas took two years.

Before we knew it, it was 2005 and we were saying our goodbyes and boarding a plane to Australia, the land of hope.

Who would have believed that we would even

make it out of our homeland alive?

CHAPTER 12

A Dream Becomes a Reality

The journey to Australia took us three days. Yes, that's right, three days! For someone like me who had never seen a plane, let alone been on one, it was a terrifying experience.

On the first day of this dream journey to the land of hope, we boarded a big, metal fish-looking thing to France. This fish-looking thing was said to fly in the air, and I was rather scared of the thought of myself in the sky. Who knew that not all fish swam in water? Some liked to fly. My seat was next to the fisheye, or window.

I could not stop looking outside as we travelled through the clouds. It was night and it seemed like I could reach out and touch the stars from where I sat. The city lights gleamed like tiny dots below us. It was a truly magical experience for me. I do not even know if I fell asleep or looked out the window all night.

The next morning, we landed in an airport in France. We needed to transit but first had to walk from the fish to a bus. We had to wait in a queue, and I had just stepped out to the open. blue sky for the first time after hours inside the fish.

Two steps further, and I immediately turned to run back inside the fish. I was both shocked and afraid at the same time. My mother immediately grabbed me and smiled softly. "What is it, my boy?"

My frantic response had been, "There is white stuff falling from the sky. It's so cold, Mama." That was my first time seeing snow and the mentality was that if something strange was happening, you had to first run to safety.

Whatever this strange white stuff was, I didn't know. All I knew was that it scared me, and it brought the coldest sensation to my body. I had never felt anything like it.

Everyone, including the flight attendants, smiled, and tried to allay my fears. After some time, and after seeing that others were not harmed in any way, I summoned the courage to step outside and dash into the waiting bus.

This bus took us to another fish. Only this time, this fish was far larger and longer than the previous one. Again, my seat was next to the window, and I kept myself busy by watching the sky as we took off. High up, I could see that we were surrounded by flying white stuff.

"Mama, is that water?" I asked.

My mother replied, "No, it's the clouds."

On this second flight, I had to deal with nausea. My stomach could not cope with being in the air for two days straight, so I dealt with constant throwing up and the occasional light-headedness.

We eventually arrived in England after a few hours. This was the country my people back home referred to as 'abroad' or 'overseas'. You see, the majority of my people only knew countries such as America, Canada, England, and Australia as the few countries that were overseas. These were usually countries in which someone had a relative.

Once we were out of our plane, we headed to the airport again to wait for our final flight. As we walked into the terminal, we approached what seemed like moving stairs. Everyone walked forward and on it to travel up a level.

Things were strange in this country, and I had seen a lot of new things in the last few days. Determined not to show my fear, I joined the crowd and hopped on the stairs while holding on to the railing with all my strength. As the motion propelled me forward, the stairs under my feet vibrated, and nervousness filled me from inside. Thankfully, I made it to the end of the stairs without any episodes, but that was not the case for my mother. She was still below the escalator, which we called moving stairs, and was refusing to get on. Everyone was busy coaxing and convincing her to step on the stairs. It took several minutes before she finally agreed. She hung onto the railing as fearfully as I had. At least I was not alone. Even the adults were afraid.

The wait for our next flight took approximately two hours. All of us sat on the comfortable airport chairs and waited patiently. There was so much to see.

This was a country I had only heard stories of, so I made sure to digest as much as I could before we had to board our next flight.

By the time we were checked in and settled on the plane for our final flight to Australia, I was too tired to stare out the window. I sat next to my mother and placed my head on her shoulder. "Are we almost there, Mama? "I asked sleepily.

My mother rubbed my head gently and rocked me slowly like a baby being put to sleep. "Yes, we are. Yes, we are." My mother's soft whisper of assurance was the last thing I heard before I surrendered to sleep.

I can see it clearly.

It's a late Friday afternoon and my partner, my son, and I are on a hike. There is a hill next to the town of Madina with grass the colour of gold. We are sitting on one of the hills watching the beautiful sunset with the winds gently brushing over our skin—a soft breeze. Around us, there are beautiful animals like giraffes and zebras. A few hours later, we head home, singing a song that feels strangely familiar. We wave and skip about with delight and bliss until we step into the town.

Something sinister lurks and I can suddenly feel the excitement drain from my body. Something bad is about to happen and I can feel it. The sky immediately turns dark, and it begins to rain. The beautiful sunset is gone, replaced with the dark sky of doom. There is something on the grass ahead of us, and I believe it is a person. With my heart pounding fast, I slowly step one foot onto the grass, leaning in to confirm my fears.

I am right! Indeed, a person is there, but the body is devoid of skin and rutted by burrowing insects. My eyes bulge wider with shock and fear.

I yell to my partner and son. I tell them to stop. We'll take a different route. Something is wrong here.

And then, somehow, we are in the village. This time, I see my mother sitting outside on a small wooden chair with my uncles standing around her. I cannot find my father. He must be inside the house.

Turning to my mother, I ask, "What is happening here? What is—"

My mother cuts me short. "A sacrifice needs to be made," she replies with watery eyes.

"We have decided to choose you for that," a voice continues from behind me. It is one of my uncles. I turn around quickly and walk towards our backyard. I walk in the direction of the rotten body, but they begin to follow me.

I see my father step outside. Good, now Papa will stop these men, *I think. But my father merely stands helpless.*

My mother sobs quietly. "I cannot save you, my son." I can hear the helplessness in her voice. "This decision has been made by some powerful people."

My adrenaline kicks in and my first instinct is to run. I want to run for safety back into the hills and forests, but instead, my legs are firmly planted in place. It is as if I am being hypnotised.

Slowly, I will myself to move and walk towards my father. My legs are heavy, and sweat is trickling from my neck down my back. I open my mouth to reply but my voice trembles as I speak.

"You guys must be crazy. I know powerful people have made this decision but...   but...this is crazy. Even though I know that the town is surrounded and that I cannot escape...this is not happening."

I walk away from him as calmly as I can while looking for safety in the opposite direction. Before anyone realises my plan, I sprint away from our compound with adrenaline enhancing my pace. But running away brings me to a crowd. A crowd celebrating my death.

The entire town is gathered, and one person must be a sacrifice, lest everyone else be killed. Just as the realization that I ran into a trap dawns on me, the crowd recognises me as the sacrifice. A crowd of people pursue me as I sprint away.

Every path or route I choose is barricaded with cruel soldiers, except no one is shooting at me. It is almost as if they are stationed there, not to kill me, but to ensure I am captured alive.

With the crowd closing in on me, I helplessly sprint a few meters before I am captured. It is too late. There is no way I can escape the village—not with the soldiers blocking every path.

I can feel the hands—hundreds of hands grabbing me at the same time. I close my eyes and shudder with fear. They take me to the soft, golden, dry grassy area in the village and tie me up. I refuse to cower silently. Violently opposing their actions, I struggle with my captors screaming and thrashing about. That does not stop them, though. And in a matter of moments, the grass is engulfed in a blazing orange flame.

Oh my God! I am going to burn. These people are going to burn me alive! I am screaming loudly and helplessly as the hungry flames crawl steadily to me.

"No! No! No!" My screams are endless. My breathing is frantic and loud.

A hand was tapping me repeatedly and I could hear a voice yelling. As I opened my eyes, I saw my mother's brown eyes staring at me with concern.

"It's okay," she said. "Breathe. Calm down."

My eyes darted nervously around me. There was no fire. It was all a dream. More accurately, it was a nightmare. This was the second time it had happened.

When I was calm and could breathe again, I noticed the curious glances and stares directed at my mother and me. But that was the least of my worries. My body was still drenched in sweat, and I was disoriented. It felt like I had run a mile. My mother continued to rock and comfort me, patting my back as she rubbed my head. "You're safe now…"

And that was it. Slowly but surely, my breathing returned to normal, and the shivers subsided. I was okay at last. Or so I thought.

CHAPTER 13

2005: Our First
Year in Australia

Throughout the whole journey, I felt like I was in another world. The food was different, and everything looked surreal. On the plane, because it had been a long, first-time journey, I was worried and uncomfortable. But not the other passengers. People were moving around inside the fish. They were walking as if they were on land, and I was simply too afraid to stand. How could I stand in the sky?

When we were offered food, I was too excited about being served by a white person that I didn't understand the menu she called out. So I went along with the last word that came out of her mouth. I was mesmerised by how beautiful she looked and how long her hair was. It was a shiny golden colour, packed neatly on her shoulders. She had a beautiful smile, too.

So, when she asked me if I wanted tea or coffee, I again went with the last thing she said. The golden-haired lady looked beautiful, but the food she served me did not. It looked strange, like baby food sprinkled with salt.

And as for the coffee, it had been a mistake. I had admired the lady up until the point when I tasted the bitter, dark liquid she so sweetly poured into my cup. It reminded me of some medicine that my mother would give me back home. How could she smile at me after giving me something so terrible?

My stomach felt heavy with gas, and I had to use the toilet. I had never been in one before. Seeing such a design, I had no idea whether to sit, stand, or even lie on it. My whole life, if we had to poop, we went to the bushes far away from the house. I could not relieve myself on this strange seat with a hole despite having attempted several times. In the end, I gave up. I would relieve myself when we got to land.

And land we did. For in a few hours, the wheels of our plane slowly glided on the tarmac of the Australian airport. We were here! At last, we had made it! On November 8, 2005, at 7:25 pm, we finally arrived in the country of hope: Australia.

Words cannot begin to describe how we felt upon arriving in Australia. I was worried that my mother would not recognise my sister and we would be stuck waiting. My mother calmly assured me that she would definitely recognise Abbigail, which dispelled my fears.

"A mother duck always knows her little ones regardless of how many others are around. She is my daughter." With that, I had been temporarily relieved.

As we walked through the halls, the sight of the security men in uniforms at Sydney airport made me begin to shake. My heart was beating fast, and my feet felt light, like I was about to run. The men reminded me of the rebel soldiers. My mother sensed my fears and grabbed my hands, warmly trying to soothe me. "Everything is okay. You're safe now."

And just like magic, my fears calmed down. This was my mother's superpower. She knew exactly what to say and how to say it. With my hand firmly locked in hers, we walked out of the airport halls into the crowd and out into the city that we had only seen in our dreams.

There were so many people. Many were smiling and holding card signs up while others held beautiful bushes, which I later found out were called flowers. What would my sister look like? How would she feel? Would I even know my sister? All these questions were running through my mind as we walked through the gates.

When I looked up, a beautiful, tall lady was looking straight at me with tears running down her red cheeks. I instantly felt warm. Instinctively, I turned around to look at my mother's face and something within me told me that she was my blood. I made the first move. I walked toward her, then broke into a small run. I reached her before anyone else could.

And then I let the tears pour as I hugged my sister, Abbigail, for the very first time in my life. I was 17 years old.

CHAPTER 14

Racing Against Time

They say time is free to spend, but expensive to get back. Time makes a lot of difference in our lives whether we realise it or not. I happened to be on the losing side. I had lost a lot of time.

Reflecting on my personal journey has profoundly shaped my ideas, lifestyle, and goals. There are several factors that have made me into the man I have become: my family, my responsibilities, my friends, and the civil war in Sierra Leone.

I was raised during the Sierra Leone Civil War. I spent most of my childhood, from 1991-2002, immersed in the war and all my memories were about wartime experiences. I saw and knew people that had to change their identities and lose their family members. I saw people lose their land and property. I saw kids being taken from their parents. I saw dead bodies on the side of the road. I saw kids crying next to their deceased parents' bodies.

People walked past and offered no help. They, too, were fleeing for their lives and did not wish to have any extra responsibility that would slow them down. All these experiences have affected most of my family and friends' mental health, and they still suffer with it now.

Though the war was over, the nightmares remained. Like the scars of a wound, they still ran deep, even though the wound was healed. The horrors and the trauma of the atrocities committed during the eleven-year Sierra Leone Civil War are indelible like a bad stench or stain. And no shower could wash it off, no matter the length. I had to learn this the hard way. But there has to be more to life than what I have experienced. Without my childhood adversities, I may not have been this determined. Perhaps this was all part of God's plan for me.

I knew this the moment I landed in Australia. I do not know what, who, when, or where, but I could feel it in my bones. I had to pursue something more.

And pursue I did!

Before going into mainstream school, I needed to attend an intensive English centre. My first day at school was strange, to say the least. I could definitely say that my school life in this new country was different and much better than my previous schooling experiences. Back home, I was in and out of school because of the civil war.

Before starting school, we had already decided that it would be better for me to go to an intensive English centre to assist in my language skills before I began mainstream schooling. It was difficult because I had to go through some tests first. It wasn't that the tests were difficult, but it was a bit strange for me since I had not undergone that sort of academic testing in a while. During the test, I had all kinds of thoughts running through my head. Is this what I really wanted? Would I face the same obstacles here that I encountered back home? The questions were endless.

At the same time, I knew that I needed to make good use of this opportunity. In this new place, education was free. Back home, only the privileged got the opportunity to attend top-range schools. Since I was a young child, it was instilled in me that education is the key to success. Having a good education, an opportunity to live with my family, and adequate support from my new teachers became a new priority for me.

The facilities for a good education in Sierra Leone could never be compared to that of Australia. Back in Freetown, there were sometimes 45-60 students in a small, confined space with barely enough room to move. Whereas in Australia, the classrooms were clean, spacious, and the class sizes were relatively small. The students were in a pleasant environment that enabled them to focus on their studies.

In Australia, I had the opportunity to go to school while staying with my family, which is something I greatly cherished. In Freetown, my school was miles away, so I had to live away from my immediate family so I could go to school more easily. It was a tedious and heart-breaking experience. I remember coming home for holidays to see my mother and siblings, having happy times with them, and then having to bid them farewell when it was time for the school to reopen. I had to leave them and go back to where I was being housed. Indeed, this new country came with so many things to be grateful for. Things I could previously only dream about.

However, this new chapter was not completely without its own difficulties. At this intensive English centre, things were a bit tough to begin with. I had no friends to interact with and had difficulty understanding the teachers, so I felt lonely. But as time went on, I soon adapted to my new environment. I joined support groups run by the school, which provided me with the necessary equipment to further enhance my reading and writing skills. I also met new people, like my best friend, Nim. It was at that point that I started to enjoy school life.

My circle of friends began to grow daily and, of course, with that came both positive and negative influences. On a positive note, I made friends who encouraged me to study, and we would do assignments together. Other friends, however, would encourage me to skip school and hang out in shopping centres and cinemas.

The choice was down to two: either be the good kid who always comes to class and does the right thing or be the 'cool' kid—someone everyone likes. I struggled desperately to be both. I didn't know how or when to compromise. The turning point came when I moved to a new class at the beginning of the academic year. I had a new teacher, who I nicknamed 'The Enforcer' because of her ability to push students to do their academic best. She motivated me to work to be my best and constantly pushed me to do better.

She invested so much time and effort in me that it changed something in me. I had never had a teacher take so much interest in my schoolwork before. Back home, if we did not do our homework or failed a subject, we would be caned by teachers and sent home to our parents. In this new country, and in this school, this teacher provided me with a second chance. She believed greatly in my potential and helped me gain confidence in my abilities.

This growth mindset led me to work extra hard, attend all my classes, and complete all my assessments—on time, too. When faced with difficulty, I did not let it deter me. I would take the initiative to find assistance and engage in meaningful discussions during and after school.

Slowly but surely, the results became visible. I am not sure how, but gradually, I became a magnet. Everyone was drawn to me. I was no longer the shy, invisible, black kid who just migrated to a foreign country. I was becoming a well-known boy among the teachers, students, and even the ladies at the canteen. I was in the mini breaching course (MBC), the equivalent to year ten in mainstream schools.

When it was time to vote for the student representative, everyone turned to me with the expectation to represent them. When the votes came in, I was elected as the student representative of the entire student body.

This new privilege led me to be more responsible. I had to be a good role model for my friends and the entire student body. I attended regular meetings with the teachers and students to discuss plans for the school, and liaised with the PE teacher, Mr. Thompson, to facilitate soccer tournaments, basketball competitions, and athletics.

Life was going great at school. I was popular, smart, and the man of the moment. But change was coming, and I was very worried about how much it would affect me. It was time for me to go to the mainstream high school. In this new world, I was not the popular kid anymore.

In my current school, the intensive English centre, most of my classmates were migrant students with similar struggles. Now, I was moving to an environment where most of the students, if not all, were born and raised in Australia.

"You are my little hero," my mother assured me on the night I confided in her about my fears.

———✦———

2008 - The second mountain: mainstream high school.

I have said this before, and I always will. My mother always has the best things to say to me.

"You did it before and will do it again. Go be the man you are destined to be." Hearing those words coming from my only mentor, and the most important person in my life, motivated me. Her faith in me made the transition to my first mainstream high school a little easier.

Again, I faced the same challenges I had previously encountered, but my experience made me understand that I just needed to focus on my schoolwork. Friends would come later.

In my subject selection, I selected Retail as one of my subjects. It gave me something different and less demanding compared to my other subjects like Economics. But even this did not quite help me as I expected.

A month and a half into the first term, I had no motivation to keep going. Unlike my former experience, this teacher was less supportive. It was not an environment in which I thrived. I was gradually becoming discouraged and less focused.

For the first few tests in Retail, I scored a 62%. My average score across all my subjects was even lower than this. It was still a top mark since I transferred to this new school, but I was not satisfied. I knew I could do better. I never forgot my accomplishments in my former school and wanted to do something that I would be proud of. No one in my family had ever reached the university level of education, but my expectation was to get to that level and become either a doctor, lawyer, or engineer.

I met a teacher, Mr. Brown, in this new school, Wyndham College, who helped shape my life.

I asked to be moved to Legal Studies. I flunked the first test, which determined whether I would be able to catch up in the class, since I had missed a few months. Undeterred, I pleaded with Mr. Brown, the Legal Studies teacher, to allow me to retake the test.

This time, I went home a desperate kid. I studied for several days and nights. Finally, I did the retake.

The result was nothing exceptional. I got a 50%, barely passing. This was not enough to convince the principal to allow me to transfer classes, but my determination had caught Mr. Brown's eye.

Mr. Brown was hopeful of my potential and offered to give me some extra help. So, with that, I gained a private tutor for both Economics and Legal Studies. The curriculum was challenging for a transfer student like me, and I struggled to complete assessments, meet deadlines, and maintain passing scores in the class. I was working twice as hard to be able to compete with the other students in my grade.

As much as I may have seemed addicted to hard work and academics, I did not live a boring social life. I don't know how I was able to balance that, except that I constantly reminded myself about my priorities and simply made sure my social life did not hinder other important areas of my life. After all, I did not come to Australia to merely have fun. I had barely made it out alive—and that I would never forget.

My friends introduced me to MSN messenger, which made communication much more accessible. It is through MSN that I met my first girlfriend, Janet. She was the most beautiful girl I had ever seen since I made Australia my new home. I told one of the boys about my interest in her and he, of course, encouraged me to ask her out.

But you see, I was a naïve young teen and asking a girl out was something I didn't have the courage to do. I kept things platonic instead and made friends with her. By that time, trouble was rocking the boat in Janet's current relationship. She was even considering leaving him. I knew this guy from the Intensive English School.

I was in Sheik the eighth child from my mother's side garage (where I was living at the time), which was converted into a bedroom, chatting with friends from Evans Intensive English Centre when a message popped up on my phone.

Today is my birthday!

It was from Janet, and I immediately replied, *Happy birthday, any plans for the big day?*

No. My boyfriend is not even able to come see me, she replied.

This was my opportunity. I realised that I probably wouldn't get this opportunity again. So, I grabbed it. We chatted for hours over MSN and after about three hours, I dropped the bomb.

Hey, do you want to meet up?

Sure! she replied.

And that was it. I jumped off my chair, grabbed my towel, and headed to the shower with all the excitement in the world.

I was halfway through my shower when I remembered that, in my excitement, I had forgotten to ask her where we would meet up. So, with wet fingers, I quickly typed out the next most crucial question.

Where do you want to meet?

Let's meet at the local park, she responded.

Great! I confirmed.

I had no idea where or how far away the local park

was. I turned to Google for help. The map estimated that the park was a 35-minute walk from my home. Not bad, I mean, I could literally walk an hour or more to get to Janet if that was all I needed to do.

I finally emerged from the bathroom smelling nice and looking squeaky clean after taking my longest shower ever. I put on my favourite K-Mart brand runners and made sure that my hair was brushed neatly. In all the excitement, I forgot to check the directions again. I paid for this mistake, for I extended my walk to an hour or more before I finally found the park.

Where could Janet be? I walked around the park, scanned everywhere, and stared at every girl who looked pretty enough to be her. And then I saw her. She was standing next to an electric street pole. She was a gorgeous girl with beautiful hair and a commanding presence. I quickened my pace, an infectious smile tugging the corner of my lips.

But this girl, she was not smiling back. And if I could see clearly, she was frowning deeply. I felt my excitement fade. Was this not the Janet I was supposed to meet?

"You're so late. I have been standing here for almost an hour," she said, clearly annoyed.

"I was lost. I am here now. Happy birthday. Do you want to go get something to eat at the fish and chips shop?"

"Sure," she replied.

And then, just like that, the frown disappeared. We sat at the park and chatted while munching our fish and chips. Hours passed and we barely noticed.

It started to get dark, and we had to head home. I was sure this was the best day of my life. Janet was smitten, and I thoroughly enjoyed her company. So, we made plans to meet up again the next day and the day after.

After a fortnight of non-stop dates, she stopped replying to my messages. I was confused. She clearly liked me enough and everything had been smooth so far.

I continued to send her messages in the morning,

afternoon, and night, but still, I got no reply.

I was very close to having my heart broken when one Saturday morning, I heard the beep of the MSN notification on my computer. I have never run faster.

It was Janet and she was trying to explain why she had ghosted me for weeks.

I'm sorry I have not been replying to your messages. I told you I was on the verge of breaking up with my boyfriend, right?

Right... I still wasn't okay with her explanation.

Well, we finally made the breakup official two weeks ago, she confirmed with a crying emoji.

That finally got me. *Are you okay?* I replied.

Yes, I just needed time.

Is this a good time to meet up now? I'm worried to death about you, I asked, taking a risk. Janet agreed, so we met up to talk about things. She seemed to be coping quite well and that meant I could shoot my shot. And shoot I did. In a few weeks, Janet and I began to date. It was from here that things began to spiral out of my control.

It was my first time being romantically intimate with anyone and it was a scary ride. She introduced me to a whole other world at such a fast pace that it both thrilled and scared me. My friends seemed to greatly enjoy my anxiety and teased me for their own amusement.

At this point, I allowed my priorities to be affected and my social life hindered other important areas of my life.

I was in year 11 of high school. In school, things started to go downhill. My grades dropped because I was too busy focusing on my girlfriend. I spent more time with Janet and less time on my schoolwork and reading. My life at home was also chaotic. Things were starting to become difficult between my family and me, more so with my elder sister, Abbigail.

I am a dreamer. I always have been. Every moment I had, I would talk about my dreams of going to university. I would talk about wanting to become a manager of a company. Most importantly, I talked about how I wanted to tell my story in the form of a film. This dream did not sit well with Abbigail. She found my behaviour and dreams to be cocky. To her, it was enough that I survived and managed to come to Australia. It was even more than enough that I was able to go to high school. She saw any further dreams besides this as obnoxious and unattainable.

But I have always been strong-willed. The more she disagreed and tried to cut me down, the more resilient I became. It was as if she was daring me to achieve my dreams and I was more than willing to take that dare.

Well, there certainly cannot be two captains on one ship. I refused to yield to her, and she was adamant, as well. Things got even worse when she learned of my involvement with Janet. The already brewing fire erupted like a volcano and several confrontations ensued. The heat continued to intensify up to the point where she asked my mother, Baida, and I to move out of her house and into Sheik's home, who also lived in Sydney, Australia. That's how the transition happened from my sister's house into Sheik's house.

We were shattered. Everyone had become so used to living with Abbigail and her family. I had final exams in a few days and moving away would be greatly disruptive for me. I decided to beg Abbigail for some more time, at least until after my exams were finished. But my sister was done, and my request was quickly declined.

I knew I was responsible for the rift we were now experiencing at home, and everyone was tense with me. It did not take long for another big conflict to break out. This time, it was me versus everyone in my family. I had to marry Janet. That was their demand. Our religious beliefs were very strict when it involved a man and a woman dating.

I strongly refused. No one would force me into marriage. On the night before my final exams, I left the house. It was 9 pm and getting late. I had nowhere to go after the argument with my family. All my friends either lived with their parents or someone else.

The local park was my only option. I found a park bench and sat alone in the dark and reminisced on the events of the past weeks. Eventually, I dozed off. The next time I opened my eyes, the warm early morning sunshine was gleaming on my face. My heart raced as I remembered my exams were in a few hours.

It was the morning of my first high school exam, and there I was, sleeping on a park bench when I should have been preparing to go to school. I paused briefly to wash up at the local religious centre and hopped on the school bus, barely making it to the stop on time.

It was on this bus that I began to mentally revise the content I'd been preparing for each subject. The first two subjects passed quickly, and my next papers were spread throughout the rest of the week and a half. I explained the situation to Nimish, a friend from school. He sympathised with me and offered to let me stay in his family's garage until I finished my exams. He warned me, however, that there was no bed.

I accepted his offer in a heartbeat. The war had prepared me for these moments. Sleeping on the floor with just a blanket was a luxury for me compared to what I had experienced in the past. Nimish and I studied the same subjects except for two, so I was able to study with him. At the end of my exams, I thanked Nimish's parents for allowing me to stay with them and returned home.

My relationship with Janet had taken a few blows from both families at this point. My girlfriend's father was against his first daughter dating someone from my race and religious background. It was later explained to me that part of that anger came from her ex-boyfriend, who was also African and the cause of her leaving home. At this point, we felt like the world was against us.

My brother's place was the only shelter I had, and even there, I was constantly dealing with my family's opposition. I made it my goal to change my girlfriend's father's perspective of me, thinking it would reunite him with his daughter. I was trying to broker peace between them, but her father had made up his mind. Janet could only return home if she stopped dating me.

At this stage, it was clear that both families would never compromise, so we decided to work hard to beat the odds against us. The first step was to try and get a job. I was nothing more than a fresher out of high school, but that did not stop me. I applied online and in person every day for different job opportunities.

Sometimes, the effort was not enough. Despite multiple applications and my determination, I could not land even a single interview.

In the end, the only opportunity I could get was a traineeship at a cleaning firm with minimum wage pay. I took it with gratitude. At last, I decided to move out and rent my own place. After several weeks of searching, I finally landed a one-bedroom apartment that was close to my brother's home, about 20 minutes away.

I had broken free like a caterpillar becoming a butterfly, but would flapping my newfound wings be easy? I had no idea. All I knew was that I had tasted freedom and it felt very good, at least at first. If things would later go sour, at that very moment, I did not care at all. Isn't it wonderful, what the desire to be free can do?

CHAPTER 15

Changes

My life was not great at this point, but I was doing okay. I had just moved out on my own for the first time and was no longer living with my family— my strongest support system. This was a big deal to me.

Meanwhile, my girlfriend was having issues with her own living situation and after a while, we both decided it would be best for her to move in with me.

So, my garage-converted suite became a home and a place where we would both experience one of the biggest changes of our lives.

Deep down, I was worried and scared. I knew that I was in no way ready for this turn our relationship was taking. But what could I do? At first, it was exciting and very spontaneous moving in with Janet. We were planning our whole lives. The sky was the limit. I encouraged her to go back to school, get a job, and pursue a career. This was very challenging for her. She attended a different school and had left school a few years ago, but I was determined to support her. I tutored her and helped her get assignments done, which resulted in a few sleepless nights. We continued this routine for a couple months until one Saturday morning in the spring.

The sun was shining brightly that morning. I walked outside with no shirt on, stretched my arms up, and let out a huge yawn. It was a typical, lazy weekend morning. Janet and I had planned to meet up with some friends for a barbeque at the Royal National Park, which had the most beautiful beach—Wattamolla Beach.

I heard her voice. Janet was calling me from inside. I quickly rushed in to see her. As I entered, I noticed her sitting at the foot of our bed with both feet firmly placed on the ground. Her eyes turned to me immediately as I entered. I could see the dark circles underneath her big, brown eyes, a sign that she had not slept much during the night. Doubling my steps, I went around the foot of the bed and dropped to my knees beside her. "What-what is wrong?" I inquired.

I placed my hands on her thighs and looked directly into her eyes. She whispered softly, "I'm tired a lot these days. I crave unusual foods. I have a weird sensation in my tummy."

I could see that it was serious, so I immediately panicked. We needed to see a doctor. I took out my red Nokia E63 mobile phone and dialled a number. It was one of our friends.

"We will not be coming to the barbeque; something just came up." Before he could respond, I hung up.

I rifled through the pile of clothes on the floor and grabbed a singlet. We hopped into the car. Our destination was a medical centre in Blacktown, at a doctor Janet introduced me to. It was a ten-minute drive from our home. Janet had introduced me to Dr. Naird. She had been their family doctor for years. She was a female Muslim doctor who shared the same religious beliefs as me. It did not take us long to pull into the parking lot of the house-converted medical centre.

As soon as Janet was called into the examination room, I stood quickly. My legs were shaking nervously. But Janet was not having it. She placed her hand on my chest and stopped me from going forward.

"I will be out soon. I want to do this by myself."

It was clear I did not have a choice here. She did not want me inside the room. This further heightened the tension. So, with blinking eyes, a clenched jaw, and disbelief, I paced about desperately, willing myself to stay calm. I had to respect her wishes.

I do not know how long I waited outside. All I can remember are the events that followed. Soon, the door opened, and Janet came out with a white stick that looked like a testing kit. I could see that there were two purple lines on it. She was stuttering as she spoke. "I-I am pregnant."

A light switch went off in my head. I could not believe what she had just said. "Pre-pregnant?"

It was my turn to stutter. I managed to reach the wall slowly and I collapsed heavily onto my seat. I put my hands on my head.

Impulsively, I stood, went downstairs to the car, and slammed the door. I needed some air. I had to get away. Janet came down the stairs after me. She took big, heavy steps and made a lot of noise. She stormed towards the car with anger visible in her eyes.

"You don't have to be part of this pregnancy! F*ck off if you want! I have a hormonal disorder. This is common among women my age." Janet sometimes had infrequent and prolonged menstrual periods, but I never knew. She tilted her head to the right and exhaled before locking her eyes with me. Then, she softly whispered, "I have a condition called polycystic ovaries. The doctor said with this condition, it is hard for me to have a baby, and this one is a miracle."

A miracle? Well, I was too busy thinking about what

this miracle would mean for us. And no matter how hard I thought, I did not feel any better.

A week after our visit to the medical centre, I was still uneasy. It was hard to eat properly, sleep, or even go to work. My mind was constantly worrying and overthinking. This is it! This is how I end. My family would be devastated and, of course, would demand that we keep the child and get married right away. Janet's family would disown her. This was how my dreams would end!

Having an abortion came up in one of our arguments, but my faith and religion, Islam, frowned upon such things. We were in a fix. We knew we could not support this child. We were barely surviving ourselves. Worse still, our families would never accept this child if we did not get married, and I was not sure if I even wanted to marry Janet. I lost over 5 kg, and Janet lost around 7 kg from the stress. Day and night, we continued to ponder about whether to abort the life growing inside her.

Finally, after two weeks of blaming, swearing, smashing things, and tears, we made a decision. We did not have money, experience, or commitment to raise this child together. So, we drove to the abortion clinic in our red 1989 Toyota Corolla. Anxiety about what we were going to do consumed us both. For the entire 40-minute drive to and from the clinic, neither of us said a single word to each other. And, from then on, Janet and I would never completely return to what we once were—two people who loved each other fiercely.

After that, time seemed to fly quickly, and soon, we were months past this ugly experience. One spring morning, our friend, Tim, and his girlfriend joined Janet and I on a road trip. The sky was clear and the breeze from the window was refreshing. We were all jolly, humming along to the music in the car as I drove. Tim suddenly requested that I turn down the music a bit. It was an unusual request, one that evoked silence among us as soon as it was uttered.

"We are getting married!"

My eyes popped open in surprise. Then, I turned to the couple with a warm smile. "CONGRATULATIONS! I am so happy for you!" I began, only to be cut off by Janet's mumbling.

"At least you have the balls to propose," she said.

Her reaction brought on an awkward silence. I quickly tried to salvage things. "Do you guys have a date yet?" I inquired a bit too cheerfully, ignoring Janet, who was busy rolling her eyes. The conversation shifted towards the new couple and the plans they were making for their wedding ceremony.

From then on, whenever someone mentioned getting married or having a child, Janet would be sure to send some spiteful remark my way.

Things at work were getting tough. Travelling to and from work was killing me. It was a typical nine-to-five routine, and it was exhausting. I returned to work for the cleaning company as an office assistant. My mate, Ethan, informed me about a job in the community services industry. I would be working with people who had disabilities, including mental health.

The working hours were flexible, and it had a convenient paycheque. Ethan was the type of guy that everyone wanted around. He was a typical guy to the boys, but a troublemaker with the ladies. A mutual friend introduced us. Ethan and I became fast friends and eventually, we did everything together. He is one of those guys you meet today, are best friends with tomorrow, and hate the next day.

I quit my apprenticeship in pursuit of this new career. A career that brought back memories of my brother, Musa. I remember going into my first shift feeling anxious about what to expect. Would it be just like taking care of Musa? Would it bring back too much pain?

I had so many questions and only a short amount of time before my first shift began, which only heightened my anxiety. By 6 am, I was introduced to a client who suffered from a mental health condition and other health issues. Among various things that stood out, the most significant aspect was his struggle with depression. It broke my heart, and my eyes immediately began to water. These were emotions I could relate to, and I knew this was an opportunity to make a difference. It was this sense of commitment that made me start my new job.

A few months down the track, a crushing blow was delivered to me. I did not score high enough on my

Australian Tertiary Admission Rank (ATAR) to make it into university. I was devastated. This was a dream I had sacrificed so much for. It was the only option I had given myself. Anything less than that meant failure. It would mean letting not only myself down, but also my mother who believed in my dream.

With a sense of helplessness, I plunged into the disability sector full time. My dedication caught the attention of my manager, who later became like a second mother to me. She decided to take it upon herself to change my perspectives on life and education. In a heart-to-heart discussion with her, she shared her own personal experiences with me to motivate and encourage me. She said, "I am not a university graduate, but I run the whole department."

That piqued my curiosity. I was eager to know how she did it without a university education. From then on, she helped me explore different ideas and career paths that I could use on my path to success.

"I admire your desire to succeed and your resilience in not letting your past ruin you," she said, taking a deep breath for emphasis. I knew what she would say next would hold very deep meaning to her, so I listened carefully. "Let me share a personal story with you," she began. And that was it. The beginning of a story that changed my thinking and reshaped the way I saw life. According to Sandra, even though she had everything—a family, a roof over her head, a car, savings, and never having to worry about food—she still felt empty most times. There were times when she experienced lengthy bouts of sadness and hopelessness. She even explained that there were periods when she battled fatigue, lost interest in work, and even struggled with suicidal thoughts. That did it for me. It then dawned on me that there was no perfect life. There never would be. And that it was perfectly normal to have struggles.

CHAPTER 16

Scars of the War

Since I was raised during the Sierra Leone Civil War, I spent most of my childhood in the war and all my memories were about wartime experiences. I've known families who have lost everything. They've lost everything that they have ever owned, and they lost people they loved. And I never forgot these images, even as time passed. There were people who felt helpless when they saw others in need. Even though they wanted to help, they themselves needed to survive, and saving others could have put their own lives at risk.

Every day, the priority was trying to stay alive to see another day. As a result of the nightmares and the trauma of these atrocities committed during the eleven-year civil war, I struggled to understand the notion of sadness when you had food to eat. I was driving home from work and thinking about my conversation with Sandra earlier that day.

I reached home by 10 pm and went straight to bed with everything still fresh on my mind. Then, it happened again. The nightmares that tormented me ever since I was a boy had returned.

It is 5 am in Madina. I am getting ready to go to school. Before school, my mother warms the rice and cassava leaves and shares it with my brother, Musa. The breakfast is not even enough for one person, but it is all we have. My mother is without wrinkles. She has that movie-star look, not too tall and willowy, but more like an action star. Her bone structure is perfect. Her skin is like silk and radiates an intelligent beauty. I look down at my feet, then my brother's, and I notice that we have no shoes. The notion of lunch doesn't exist. We start school at 8 am and walk bare foot for two hours. The road is full of red dust, gravel, and ground rocks. It's the mango season, and my brother and I climb the mango trees to get ourselves food.

"Musa! We are running late," I yell. Rushing down the mango tree, we slide down the rough branches. We had taken off our shirts and used them as wraps around our palms as we climbed. Six feet from the ground, we jump and land on our feet. We wipe the dry wood off our stomachs. There is no time. I urge Musa forward.

We grab our plastic bags that serve as school bags, and we begin to run. We run for about 20 minutes before we make it to the school compound. Everyone is already lined up for the morning assembly. We are late! So, we face punishment. The teacher asks us to squat 100 times and gives us a dozen lashes when we are done. Musa and I turn to each other knowingly. A smile forms at the corner of his lips. No punishment could take away the joy we feel that we have enough mangoes to eat for lunch. Food! We have food to sustain us for the remaining six hours we have to spend in school. How can we possibly be sad?

By 3 pm, our ordeal at school is over. We are on our way home. As we walk back, we devise a way to entertain ourselves. We play sock soccer—we put leaves inside a sock and make it look like a ball. It is all fun until disaster strikes. I miss the sock and end up kicking an in-ground rock, which pulls off my big toenail in the process. The pain is indescribable. The pale, white flesh of my big toe, where my nail originally was, now stares emptily at me. My eyes are wide as I scream. I flap my hands in pain and hop frantically on my other good foot. I am not crying. The pain is beyond tears. This one shakes my soul.

Musa immediately removes the leaves using the sock as an emergency first aid plaster for my injured toe. We walk the way home in silence. I'm in pain. We could not tell anyone at home. If you play football and get injured, you get spanked. I decide to endure the pain quietly. No one, not even my mother, would know.

A week later, Musa and I were playing a game of chase and run from the front door to the backyard. I accidentally kick the wooden front door with my wounded big toe!

I let out a piercing scream and jumped out of bed drenched in sweat.

From primary school age, we were taught that if you're hungry, you find something to eat, and if you're sad, you find something you like. Whether it is playing soccer, visiting friends or family, or dancing under the rain—find something that makes you happy. You're totally responsible for changing the way you feel. Being exposed to mental health struggles at work took me back to my childhood and led me to dream about reuniting with my best friend, my brother, Musa.

I struggled to understand this concept. For people who still live in Sierra Leone, mental illnesses, like PTSD and schizophrenia, are considered the devil's work or the work of evil spirits. This is a standard way of thinking. Most people with mental health conditions believe in traditional methods to cure their mental illness, as they think an evil spirit causes mental illness. However, conventional pharmaceutical methods of mental health care are the only solution for most patients.

Furthermore, some Sierra Leoneans believed that

mental health problems were caused by witchcraft curses, or bad people within the family. Others thought it was a curse from God. The native juju man would say: "The evil is within you—sacrifice a goat, sheep, or cow, then the evil spirit will be transferred to the animal." I once held this belief. That was until I migrated to Australia and met August.

August had been a one of my good friends since my arrival in Australia. I met him through my local soccer team. Many times, I wanted to slap him and make him realise that he had no reason to be sad! He had been sad since I met him, but I never really noticed.

I didn't take him seriously until he told me that, in the past, he had been so sad that he had suicidal thoughts. I started to research and read more about this kind of sadness. That was how I learnt about depression. I learnt that I, too, was dealing with it although I was ignorant of it at that time. The more I learnt, the more I saw the need for it to be addressed.

And now, with Sandra's help, I was beginning to fully open up to critical mental health concepts. Although I was reluctant to enrol in a tertiary education course, Sandra convinced me that it would broaden my intellect and help me decide what I would like to do in the future. I completed several TAFE courses and, before I could complete one of the other courses, I received more news. I was finally granted admission to university. But now, I had more responsibilities than before. How on earth was I going to juggle a full-time job, a relationship, and getting a university degree?

CHAPTER 17

Surviving Racism

I survived the eleven-year Sierra Leone civil war; I'll survive racism, too!

One thing I love to do, besides staying fit, is meditate. And with meditation comes reminiscing. Today, as I sit for a light lunch, my memories take me back to November 2005.

When I first arrived in Australia as a boy, the only people I could relate to in this first-world country were rappers like 50 Cent and Tupac. Resembling these two icons in my swag and dress style was the coolest thing I knew. I began to consider myself part of this new community and culture rather than a refugee. Now that I think of it, though, maybe I had overdone the swagger a bit too much. But, to my boyish mind then, I considered myself first class.

One Saturday in summer around midday, I went out dressed in my favourite baggy jean shorts with a large Tupac face embroidered on my right thigh, a white singlet, and an ultra-stretch white head wrap. A younger version of the men I admired. *Nobody could touch this drip*, I thought to myself.

I was standing at Blacktown railway station waiting for the train. When it arrived, the doors opened. I stood to the side to let a group of middle-aged ladies enter first, and then I slid into the train as the doors were about to close. There were a few empty seats. I jumped to skip the first step and landed on the second step, headed to the upper level. I found an empty two-seater in the middle of the carriage. I sat at the far corner to make room for another person to sit.

We reached Seven Hills station and more people hopped on. The train stopped again at Westmead and Parramatta. The train was filled with passengers. It was a busy weekend, and everyone was commuting. The train was packed with people and a lot of them were even standing up, but the seat beside me was still empty.

As people hopped on and off the train, I quickly noticed a woman standing a few seats in front of me who appeared to be in her thirties, the same age as my sister. I softly tapped her on the elbow and said, "Excuse me, please take my seat. I'll stand." She quickly turned away from me. It felt as though the entire carriage came to a halt as her nose wrinkled, brows lowered, and the frown lines on her forehead appeared. I did not even have a clue what I did wrong.

She quickly wiped her elbow where I had touched her with a look of disgust on her face, like that of a baby who had just tasted lemon juice for the first time. The only words she uttered to me were a firm, "No! I'll stand!"

Then, it dawned on me why the seat beside me had

been empty throughout all the stops. This woman simply did not want to sit next to me. And it was not just her. Everyone else had ignored that seat too, preferring to stand all through the journey rather than share a seat with me.

I felt like a kid at school who had to sit by himself in the school cafeteria. In my culture, back in Sierra Leone, especially in the villages, we were required to give up our seats for anyone older who was standing. This was a sign of respect. Suddenly, I felt alone. It was like I was in a forest surrounded by wolves waiting to devour me. I could not wait to get off the train. The hate I saw around me scared and depressed me so much that I thought of cancelling my trip.

As soon as the train reached Central, I rushed to the door so that I was the first one to get off. I ran up the stairs and tripped at the last few steps and fell onto my knees. Embarrassed, I got up quickly and found an exit out of the building. At this point, I had endured enough of a terrible day and decided to call it quits. How was I going to get home? I would do anything but ride the train again. I called a cab to take me back to Blacktown. He wasn't the friendliest, but better than the people on the train. I reached home, went straight to my room, and lay on the floor. I looked up at the ceiling, pondering in silence about the events of the day. As a teenager, I did not know how to cope with this feeling—the feeling of not belonging and being treated like an outcast because of my colour. This ordeal had a negative effect on me. I soon began to lose who I really was.

To be accepted, I tried to alter my appearance. I started doing things like growing out and dying my hair, piercing my ears, and talking differently by changing my accent. I do not even know which accent I tried to mimic, but it definitely didn't sound Australian no matter how hard I tried. It was a waste of my time and efforts as I went through this short phase of trying to become somebody else.

In the end, I decided to keep things simple. I started buying very cheap and simple stuff. No more embroidered Tupac face or 50 Cent swagger. This hard experience introduced me to myself. Without this heartbreaking event, I would have always continued to be someone else. Before I left the house, I'd always look in the mirror and ask myself, "Is this outfit for me?"

When I met people, before I spoke, I would first make sure I believed whatever it was I wanted to say and then I would speak and communicate that in simple English with conviction and in my own natural accent. There was no need to try to be someone else when I could be a better version of myself.

As my mind returns to this situation from where I am now in 2019, I smile as I realise that on the rare occasions I ever have to use public transport to go to the office, I don't even notice if someone sits next to me or not. Half the time, I am either too busy to notice or I simply don't mind. My belief system has changed, of course. I am a 'cele-pretty'. I do not expect anyone to have the courage to sit next to me. So, I sit comfortably in my seat and tell myself that I am a 'cele-pretty', my own version of a celebrity. I wear a gentle smile on my face at all times.

Black people are known to be physically strong. Our physique is different from other races. Our chest muscles are fuller, our shoulders are broader, and our overall anatomy is larger and can seem intimidating at times. This perceived strength, which is sometimes associated with coming from African decent, seemed to stigmatise my friends and me. Even when we are just trying to enjoy ourselves, we are perceived as a threat.

We never went clubbing alone. Due to our physique, and sometimes our over excitement, it was easy to appear intimidating, especially when we went out in groups. On many occasions, especially when we were out clubbing, I have personally witnessed the security guards have real problems whenever a fight broke out in the club.

If one fight were to happen, then all the black people would be refused entrance. Our race was viewed as a whole, not as individuals. I don't drink, use drugs, or smoke, and I would never fight in a club, so why should I be refused entrance?

In Sierra Leone, all our childhood play typically included games that developed skills in understanding rhythms. We used dance as a form of communication.

Our bodies' creative movement, the timing of the beats, and the ability to use the space around us with endless energy, are among the few tools we used to communicate. We were able to identify and understand these core characteristics that are essential in communicating our message for the love of dance to other people.

Dance utilises the concept of total body articulation, so sometimes, the deliberate slow or fast movements of every part of the body with changing facial expressions are purposeful to charm the ladies. The bass is so powerful. For some people, they can feel that energy coming from all over the dance floor and our bodies respond naturally on their own with equal energy.

It was a Thursday night, and I still remember it vividly. I had just finished work heading home when one of my mates called to ask if I'd like to go out for the night. There is a venue in the heart of Sydney CBD where, at the time, weekend party kicked off early with dancing, drinks, and good times. It had four venues under the same roof with DJs playing different types of music. However, the two venues that caught my attention were the Change Room, which was spinning old school hip hop, and the Den & Lounge, which was playing RnB and hip hop.

So, at 10 pm, we wore our favourite easy-move jeans and dancing footwear and headed to the city. To get us pumped and ready for the big night out on the dance floor, we had the best old school and the latest RnB and hip-hop tunes blasting in the car. We called it the 'pre-workout'.

We arrived in the city and parked five minutes away from the club. As we were approaching the venue, we could hear the blend of different tunes. The line was about 50 meters long. We joined the queue, and I slowly moved my head and legs to the music playing from inside. I was looking forward to my glass of red bull with ice before heading to the dance floor.

I have never tasted alcohol, drugs, or tobacco in my life. Sometimes, to appear cool like everybody else, I'll get an energy drink from the bar and ask for it to be poured into a glass with ice. The colour of the drink was the same as that of alcohol, so it looked like I was also having something hard.

The queue moved slowly, and we had to stand in line for about 30 minutes. Finally, only a few meters to the door, we heard a voice from behind saying, "Boys, please step out of the line." It was the club's security guard and he had five other security guards with him. The ladies in front who were seductively eyeballing us turned together with the rest of the crowd to stare— stares of concern and interest in what would happen next. After five minutes of bullshit with the guards, the only thing we could make out was that another black person from Sydney had gotten into a fight a month ago, and now no black person was allowed in the club for three months.

Imagine punishing an entire race because one person did something wrong. White people fought in clubs too, didn't they? Yet, you'd never see them punishing every single white person.

I was bewildered. I could not believe my ears. My head was bent low, and my hands were in my pocket as I wondered why we had to endure such treatment.

We were not trying to fight anyone. We were not even the same people who had fought. We were just here to have a good time like everyone else.

And then suddenly, it dawned on me. It was their fault and not mine. The security guards were scared that my kind was powerful and that they would not be able to remove us from the club if something were to happen. I mean there wasn't really anything we could do at that point anymore. I wouldn't want to try and find *myself* in one of those dark rooms (I've been working on my dad jokes these days).

Worse still, I thought the security guards were jealous that we always had all the ladies' attention. This helped to lighten how we felt. I knew if we did not change our perception, we would continue to sulk. So, raising my head, I straightened my shoulders, took my hands out of my pockets, and gave those who were staring an infectious smile. With an air of confidence, I turned around and walked back to the car with my mates and headed home.

There would always be another club, after all.

CHAPTER 18

A New Storm Arises

I am an optimist. It is both a good thing and a bad thing. Along with it comes a very strong sense of purpose and will. I could juggle it all, or so I thought. But it seemed that whenever I thought I had everything under control, life would throw me off balance and send me back to the beginning.

It had been 12 months since the abortion. The one that had almost taken our love to rock bottom. Janet was taking her contraceptive pills regularly, so I thought. We were using the pull-out method, up until Janet's birthday. That day, we were feeling all jolly and in high spirits. We decided to go to a local restaurant for dinner and celebrate at home by ourselves. It was fun—a little bit too much fun. For as soon as we finished enjoying the birthday cake, I become aroused. As soon as she walked past me, I grabbed her hand and pushed her softly against the wall with my boner pressing against her. She responded eagerly, encouraging me. That was all I needed before the urge to be inside her completely overtook me. We made love with all we had, and in the passion, I forgot to pull out.

As we lay together that night, exhausted from the energy exertion, she informed me that she may have forgotten to take her pills sometime. We discussed getting the morning-after pill to remedy things. Janet agreed. After all, we were not ready for a baby. But little did I know, no morning-after pill was taken, and a baby was underway again.

Exactly one year after the abortion of the first child, I arrived home from work to see a testing kit on the table. Yes, Janet was pregnant again. I was both cold and surprised. Overcome with doubt, I asked. "I thought we discussed for you to take the pill?"

Her response was small. "I forgot."

I could not believe my ears. How does one forget this type of thing after having suffered an abortion only a year prior? She knew everything about me down to my finances. She knew how hard it was for us to even afford rent. We were struggling to keep things together. How could we bring a child into this situation?

Instantly, memories of the past abortion came back. I never forgot how much Janet and I suffered during the last year because of our decision. We were barely recovering and now it was happening to us again.

I had so many questions. Were we ready to become parents? Could we go through another abortion? Would I have to give up on my dreams? The questions were endless, and the answers were unclear. The only thing I was sure of was that another abortion was not an option.

---❖---

A triple threat in pursuit of lost time

Time is of the essence. When lost, you never get it back, no matter how hard you try. I remember at one stage, I had to work from 6 am to 2 pm, then I had university lectures/tutorials from 3 pm to 5 pm, TAFE classes from 6 pm to 8 pm, and then sleep for an hour and half before getting ready for an active night shift from 10 pm to 6 am. It was one of the most challenging times in my life and Janet knew this better than anyone else. I was always glued to my computer to guarantee all my units followed right after the other, as this ensured I wasted the least amount of time possible at the university, so I would still have enough time for TAFE and work.

I did all of this was because I was chasing my dream. I wanted something that was long-term. I wanted to secure a managerial position in my industry. To do this, I needed some form of qualification to increase my knowledge in my field. After much research into Management and Industrial Relations, I believed this was the major and sub-major that would set me apart from the rest.

But I did not have all the time in the world, and I was conscious of this. I was chasing lost time and every mistake took my dream further away from me.

I was undertaking a diploma in disability services at TAFE, a bachelor's degree at university, and had a job I wanted to progress in. My job allowed me to work at night. The night shifts enabled me to study and complete the assessments after I finished my tasks and the clients fell asleep.

It was a lucky deal, to be able to work and study. It was a tough time, but I was determined to hang on. My schedule meant giving up a lot of things. I was invited to university parties. I longed for fun, but fun was for people with time. I had exams coming up at TAFE, then a week later, exams at the university. Even sleep was a luxury I could not afford. I could only sleep for three hours most days and it was beginning to trouble me. I was having trouble concentrating in class. So, I started power napping for 15 minutes between my courses at the university and 30 minutes before the evening TAFE class.

Finally, the time for my TAFE assessment arrived and I was deemed satisfactory. My TAFE journey was over, and I had made it. This meant I could devote more time to my final university exams. I dived deep into it. Throughout the day and night, a book was always nearby. I came from a family of 24 siblings, yet no one had ever reached this level of education. I was going to be different.

It wasn't that I had the highest IQ or anything like that; I had simply been dedicated to succeeding and reaching my dreams. I was shameless in asking for help from co-workers, peers, teachers, and even strangers.

On the other hand, the pressure at home was mounting. Janet and I were having arguments every day. The pressure was driving me crazy. It was not too long before I spiralled towards one costly mistake.

On the morning of one of my exams, I had taken a shower, packed my study notes, and driven to the campus to find it was deserted. It was strange. The car park was full, but nobody was outside studying as usual. When I walked to the auditorium, I met a teacher standing outside. Upon inquiry, I learned that the exams had already begun an hour ago.

I was shocked to the core. My calendar read 50 minutes to the exam time. How did this happen? Apparently, I had the wrong time on my calendar. When I checked my student email, my shoulders slumped in defeat. It was over. I failed my Marketing Principles and Statistic units. I had to retake them during the summer break.

Ethan was the only friend that was there to assist Janet and calm her down whenever we had a fight. It got to a point where I would call Ethan to go to mine and Janet's place before I left work to ensure that he would be there to help diffuse any situation that may arise.

I had already confessed to Ethan that I had stopped loving Janet a few months into the relationship. I was selfish, scared of loneliness, and continued to hope things would get back to the way they were before. Ethan encouraged me to end the relationship and follow my heart, but I did not have the courage.

Unfortunately, a few months passed, and issues kept piling up until my relationship with Janet became a full-blown disaster. At this point, it was both toxic and harmful for both of us to continue our lives together. Janet became sceptical and paranoid about everything I did. Over time, she openly accused me of cheating with one of my friend's girlfriends.

I remember thinking that I was done. Done with the fights, the drama, and the whole embarrassing situation. I was done enduring, hoping things would ever be normal again. I was finally ready to end things with Janet.

But not so fast. She had my child and I owed it to her to be there for our child. She returned home with me for the last couple of weeks before she gave birth and after that, I decided I would find a way to move on from this mess I had created. Looking back now reflecting, I probably should have done things a little differently.

———— ❈ ————

Life After Azlan was Born

Janet's due date was near: the day my son, our child, would be born. That morning, we packed clothes, snacks, and baby clothes into a small bag and headed to the hospital as we were asked to by the hospital. At 3 pm, Janet began to experience cramps and contractions that lasted for over 12 hours.

Finally, on March 12, 2013, my baby Azlan was born! When I looked at him that day at the hospital, words couldn't describe the emotions I felt. He looked so much like Janet, with his nose and jaw almost identical to hers. And when I looked closer at him, I could still see a miniature version of myself. It was both a scary and thrilling emotion at the same time.

Immediately, I made a promise within myself that this child would be raised in the best conditions. I would absolutely love this child fiercely. How I was going to do that, and if I would even be able to keep such a promise, was another matter entirely.

Janet was discharged without delay, but Azlan needed to stay at the hospital for a few more days under special care. We were parents for the first time. We had made a new life together. A child that would call me Dad, and Janet, Mum.

In our excitement, our arguments and fights suddenly stopped. We were all too eager to hold our son and meet the challenges of new parenthood. We went shopping together, bought a few household essentials for the new baby, some clothes, nappies, and even a baby bed. Whatever was needed for a baby, we got it. This seemed to repair the cracks in our relationship and drew us closer. It was like we had less time to focus on ourselves. Whatever decisions we made, Azlan came first.

However, this peace did not last for long. A year later, the arguments began again. This time, they were much worse, and we had a child in the house. It broke me each time we fought. I knew I was breaking my word. This was not the home I wanted my son to be raised in. I decided to address things once and for all.

One evening, I called Janet to sit with me and talk.

When she agreed, I began the conversation as softly as possible. "Janet...the way we are now...I do not want Azlan to grow up seeing us arguing the way we are at this moment."

I desperately wanted to make things work. I had tried for years. But you can never make a relationship work out by yourself. The other person needs to put in work too or else it will always be a futile effort.

"It's...not working," I sniffed, feeling overwhelmed with emotion. "You can stay here with the baby, with everything. I'll move out and find a place to stay. I swear I'll be there all the way."

Tears filled both our eyes; we turned instinctively to look at Azlan lying on the bed peacefully. "No. I'll move out with the baby," Janet insisted. "This place has too many memories. I'd like to start fresh."

It was the summer of 2014 when I ended things with Janet. I spent the rest of the season studying and completing the remaining unit I had left. I was always the oldest student in the class. My highest score while doing my bachelor's degree was 68%, and the rest were in the 50s. Throughout high school and university, I never won any award or recognition for academic accomplishments.

———�֎———

It has always been my dream for Mother to witness the three most important events of my life —degree, wife, and house.

It has been ten years now since I arrived in Australia. How time flies. I came to this foreign country as a young boy haunted by the scars and trauma of a civil war.

By September 2015, I was about to graduate with a university degree! Yet, disbelief was still within me. A boy from a poor village in Sierra Leone, Africa was about to graduate. On that day, I invited my mother, my niece, Shishi, Azlan, and my best friend, Ethan. For a very long time, my mother used to watch parents celebrating their children's graduation on TV and had always wondered if she would get to experience it one day. She did.

On this special day, the sun was rising bright and clear, and the cool spring breeze was blowing. It was the perfect day for a graduation ceremony!

I entered the room wearing my graduation gown while the guests were seated in the auditorium. The stage was set. The first pair of eyes I saw were my mother's. Her eyes were wide open, tears of joy and admiration flowed down her cheeks. I read her lips, "You're my hero." And I have never been prouder. I've always dreamt for my mother to witness the three most important events in my life: graduating, buying my first home and one day marrying the love of my life. That day, I achieved one of those dreams.

The graduation ceremony continued. The students' names were called one by one to collect their certificates. Then, I heard it. I heard my name being called and suddenly everything came to a halt. My heart began to beat fast, blood rushed to my limbs, and I felt my adrenaline rise just like it did during my nightmares and the trauma of the atrocities committed during the civil war.

With an indescribable thrill, my feet shook, and my

palms became a sweaty mess. The only good thing about this experience was that my face was filled with a smile. I was happy. Before I reached out to collect my certificate, I turned to my mother in the crowd and whispered, "Thank you."

After the ceremony, Mother and I hugged so tight. We were both filled with gratitude and other emotions. It wasn't so much about the degree. It was about the adversities, self-doubt, loneliness, fear, heartbreak, depression, procrastination, and many more things I had to overcome to achieve this. It was about surviving the process more than the actual results. I'm far from a genius, but the war had taught me a valuable lesson: to keep going regardless and to be thankful for every win I achieved.

Looking back now, I am grateful for everything that has made me who I am today.

CHAPTER 19

The Past Still
Haunts my Dreams

T he best thing about not working on Fridays—I mean, not working two jobs back-to-back on Fridays—was that I did not have to wake up so early in the morning.

You see, I speak to my mother three times daily. Once before work, once after work, and once before bed. Yes, I am a mama's boy and proudly so. I'm usually up at around 4 am. I go to the gym, pray, write for a few minutes, and get ready for work, which starts at 6 am. On Fridays, I only work at my second job. I get to have an extra hour of sleep.

On Fridays, I am usually up at around 5 am. I pray, then head to work. One morning, I decided to give my partner more cuddles before heading to work, so I ended up leaving at 6:30 am. I dialled 0401 62—the number of my only mentor (my mother), as I did every morning on my way to work. We usually talk about my work, finance, partner, and other family members. On this day, we focused more on the family back home in Sierra Leone. I had my orphan nieces, nephews, my late brother's wife, and one close family relative under my care.

My mother and I sent money each month for feeding, schooling, and other necessities. I had become curious about how much they really needed every month, so I called and asked for the prices of everyday materials such as a bag of rice, oil, palm oil and weekly groceries cost. The total cost added up to $427 every month. I was relieved because we had been sending $500 twice or sometimes three times every month.

This month, I had sent the money on the 1st of September, and yet, on the 14th, they called and requested more money for food.

It was frustrating to me that I was working two different jobs to take care of everyone's needs, and they were asking for more than they really needed. I poured my emotions out to my mother, who shared the same frustration I did. However, she reminded me that it was twice as hard in Sierra Leone than in Australia.

Hawa, my oldest niece, had finished school a year ago and it had taken her three months longer than usual to get her exam results. Three years later, she still could not find a job. She hadn't even gotten an interview!

As we talked, my mother shared her desire to travel back to Sierra Leone. She was planning to go towards the end of the year to supervise the building project my brother and I were organizing for her.

You see, all her life, the one thing my mother had wished for the most was to have a house to call her own. She wanted it so badly—like an asthma patient wants air. At one point, she had even been reluctant to remain overseas. According to her, *'A nor want the family ose for broke,'* meaning a family house represented our family legacy. Without a family home, our family does not belong.

Earlier, Abbigail had promised her that if she came overseas, within a year or maximum two, she would build my mother a family home. You see, building back home is expensive. If you are lucky and have the right kind of people, it could cost you a lot less. A three-bedroom home costs around 70 million SLL. However, with the exchange rate of 1.00 AUD = 7,314.8570 SLL, it could cost around $10,000 Australian Dollars to build a house and keep the family legacy alive.

My mother arrived in the land of hope in 2005. In 2018, Abbigail owned multiple properties in Australia and still had not helped our mother's dreams. It was coming to the end of 2018 and it was clear to us that she would not follow through on her promise.

I had been suspicious of the relative in Sierra Leone who was facilitating the building project. I suspected he was being dishonest and was telling us a price that was higher than the actual cost. This was because, firstly, since the building project began, all the quotes he provided had always been an even figure. Secondly, we asked him to get a quote for a generator, since there was still no electricity in some parts of Sierra Leone, and he didn't get back to me until four weeks later. I had already asked the builder to get a quote for us so I could compare the cost. After comparing the two quotes, my relative's price was $500 more than the other quote for the exact same generator!

I expressed my concerns to my mother and wondered how long this had been going on. My mother shared the same concern but again, advised me to be patient. Besides, we did not have anyone else over there to facilitate this project. I could trust my oldest niece, but since she was a woman, she could be murdered if people knew that we were sending large amounts of money to her. The project was at the final stages, so we kept our hope and patience intact. Our conversation ended on this note. I was already at the office and ready to begin another morning of meetings.

Throughout my studies and work, I have always had an internal battle with communication: both written and verbal. I always admired how people could write so well without any struggles. When writing assessments, I'd always have to use different words because, most times, the words I wanted to use were clear in my mind, I just could not spell them correctly or use them in a way that would be grammatically correct. In the end, I would have to settle for a simpler word that never seemed to completely fit. English is difficult.

My inability to fully express myself in English affected my reporting and email writing. It created fear and anxiety in me. Fear to speak in meetings and in the office when colleagues were around. Fear of being judged on my use of grammar continued to jeopardise my career. This fear inhibited my growth.

I was a Team Leader for three years. Then, my mentor urged me to apply for an Acting Coordinator role. In this role, I was able to rally several Team Leaders and coordinate them. I have a calm persona, appreciation for staff, and a kind spirit. I always want to bring out the best in people. This helped lessen problems for me at the office.

However, whenever I needed to take a phone call, my heart would beat rapidly, and I would begin to look at who was around in the office. The office had an open space full of permanent coordinators, a rostering team, HR staff, and more.

The voices in my head always told me that I should've used a better word for every word that came out of my mouth. I was cautious of everything I said and often mumbled when I spoke. How would I be able to score another career opportunity if I kept this up? I knew I had to act fast to solve this issue. When I was a child, the war had taught me to keep going even in the face of adversity.

I have been taught to keep going even when I am constantly battling with my inner voice.

I kept studying management courses and applying for management roles despite struggling with English. The constant training helped calm my speaking anxiety and my determination to quell my fears further boosted my morale. There was no position available in my current company, so I applied to another company for a managerial position.

I got the job. This was a new organisation with new systems, managers, and expectations. I inherited a diverse team with strong personalities, and this time, I was in the centre of the room. This organisation had the vision to create a world where every person is welcome. It didn't matter if someone had an accent or an English-speaking background. If you could do the job, then you were welcome.

After six months in my new position, I could barely get my team to attend team meetings. Nothing came together. The group wasn't able to produce anything lasting. What's more, the individual work of each member was more significant than when it was a team task. Some team members were frustrated and sometimes expressed that they preferred working alone. There was nothing to indicate that my group of Team Leaders were operating as a team. It was a mess, and I was in the middle of it all. Amidst the storm, I was still battling my communication problems and I was always wary of who was in the room. How could I fix someone else when I needed fixing, too?

I was the manager of this group. I needed to speak English clearly and use a wider range of vocabulary when responding to emails—or so I thought. However, even my accent annoyed me. This group all spoke perfect English with no foreign accents, and I couldn't help but begin doubting myself all over again.

I had high expectations for myself, and it seemed like I was falling short. I needed to overcome these self-doubts and lead this group to operate like a dream team where the team result would be greater than any individual work.

My confidence was in the deepest pits and my work rate was taking a big blow. This ordeal began to affect the way I communicated with the higher-ups, my fellow team leaders, and fellow managers. I was even at risk of losing my job.

And if I did, then I would have failed my mother and my brother, Musa.

That night, I returned home tired and worried. How would I deal with my anxiety at work? My overthinking mind kept replaying the scenes over and over again as I lay in my pitch-black room and tried to sleep. It was about 10 pm, and I was already in bed in a bid to have an early start as I had to wake up as early as possible for work. I remember my thoughts wandering from one place to another just before I drifted off into a nightmare. How it began, I do not know, but all I can remember is that suddenly I could see myself in a place that seemed both familiar and yet strange.

In this place, I have a wife, Elly, and my two children, August and Hayden, live with me in a three-story building that looks like a family house. My mother, my brother, Musa, my sister, Baida, and my niece, Kadijah, are on the ground level. It is a Friday evening in winter, the weather is cold, and the wind is blowing lightly. The whole family is in the yard around the campfire. The children are running around. My brother and I are roasting some marshmallows, while my mother and sister talk about family stuff.

Hours later, we all head to bed. At around midnight, I wake to gunshots. The second floor is lit up with gunshots. As I look down, I can see my family crying out for help. When I turn around, my wife and kids are also looking at me with fear in their eyes. How could we escape this and not lose anyone in the crossfire?

With August and Hayden in my arms, and Elly behind me, we run down the stairs and into the courtyard. At the midpoint of our escape, I pause and tell Elly, "You need to take the kids out of here. I need to go back in and look for my mother, Baida, and her daughter."

With tears, Elly runs away into the gardens with the children. Suddenly, I am running back to the house, but not before the soldiers spot me. Everyone suddenly turns their gun towards me to open fire! Immediately, I dive towards the nearest bushes and take cover. From my hiding spot, I can hear my family inside screaming for help. I run around the house, into the backyard, and through the back door. The soldiers realise I am back in the house, so some of them rush from the second floor down onto the ground floor, while the others stand at the railing and shoot down in my direction. My family is trapped inside the room on the other side of the house. They are so scared of coming out because they might get shot. I need to run across to the other side and into that room where my family is trapped.

I can hear the footsteps of the troops rushing downstairs, kicking and shooting the doors. It is now or *never. If I want to save my family, I must decide now, or we are going to die here. I choose to sprint to the other side. Just before I can reach the door, one of the bullets pierces through my leg. Blood is spewing like a fountain, and I am screaming from the excruciating pain. My mother opens the door just as I collapse in her arms. We huddle in a corner near the door while the gun shots increase. Bullets fly everywhere. Someone has to make a sacrifice, and instantly, I know what I have to do.*

"I am going to create a distraction for you guys. You have to run in the opposite direction. I will drag myself to the right side of the house," I inform them. I do not leave any room for objections. This is what has to be done. Everyone cannot die at the same time. I crawl to the right side of the house, screaming as loudly as possible to draw attention to myself. The bait works. The soldiers shoot in my direction but cannot get a clear shot as the darkness provides a temporary cover.

The distraction goes as planned. My family runs outside. The troops finally shoot down the door, and everyone pauses for a moment to watch me suffer. I crawl through a nearby door and make it outside. One of the soldiers targets my other leg and aims a shot. The bullet connects and I feel excruciating pain. I scream again. They kick me until I fall into a freshly dug grave. I lie on my back, six feet under, and look up at the many troops standing above me. They all point their guns down in my direction!

Someone was shaking me vigorously. I could hear my name, too. I could hear fear and the voice. I fought my way to consciousness and forced my eyes open. When they finally did, I saw who it was. My girlfriend at the time was nervously shaking me. My eyes were glistening with fresh tears.

"You-you were crying aloud in your sleep," she said, her voice breaking with emotion.

It was all a dream. It was not real, I assure myself silently.

I needed to find a way to overcome my inner voice and the doubts that I battled if I wanted to save my mother's dream and my dream. I needed to progress in my career. My experience with people with disabilities started at a very young age, since I had to care for my disabled brother. When I migrated to Australia, I was able to transfer my personal experiences with my brother to the role of a Support Worker and then to the Client Service Manager role.

I believe that my personal experience with my brother allowed me to understand the needs and wants of people living with some form of disability. So, I began to research on my own and soon found a solution. I became obsessed with learning. First, I started reading books and listening to motivational speeches. I used some of the ideas I got from the books to develop a 'how we work together' project for my team.

I wanted to build a culture that generated joy. I wanted to establish a team where we all had a sense of purpose, took responsibility, learnt from one another and continuously improved. I wanted us to achieve this through team collaboration. I wanted a team that genuinely cared about one another. If someone was struggling, for example, the others should be willing to help them out.

Caring is important, so is sharing—specifically, sharing knowledge and experiences. I wanted to facilitate a learning culture where Team Leaders could sit together and work through some tasks. That would encourage everyone to learn from each other's experiences and strengths and create more development opportunities.

My aim was to make the team more resilient and prepared for the future. I wanted to create an environment in which people continually enjoyed exchanging views, learning, teaching, and expanding their horizons. I came up with a world-class strength-based approach and turned my attention away from the areas that needed improvement. That was what intense hours of studying, analysis, and research had taught me.

I realised that there was someone else out there who had gone through a similar situation as mine. I found a book that talked about overcoming struggles with English. My personal experience was to keep going despite adversity. The ideas for this project came from the books I read. The delivery of the project? I was inspired by several motivational speeches I listened to. My manager proofread some of my important work. As I continued to develop myself, she recommended Grammarly, a paid software, to continue transforming my writing skills.

In time, I judged myself less and my confidence grew. No, I wasn't perfect—far from it—but there was visible progress. So, I learned to take joy in the little steps I took and focused more on making progress, no matter how many mistakes I made. It didn't matter how many times I fell—the point was that I got up bravely every time.

Serving others gave me the greatest joy. I worked for the best company in the world and had the opportunity to serve others and lead a dream team. I had also finally completed my mother's home, which was like a breath of fresh air after drowning in a pool of water.

Above all, I knew my brother, Musa, was proud of me up in heaven.

CHAPTER 20

Ethan, The Ride or Die Brother

After I lost my brother, Musa, and my best friend, Shaggy, in Sierra Leone, I was left heartbroken. I hadn't been able to call someone my best friend since. Ethan was introduced to me through a mutual friend. We became fast friends and eventually started doing everything together. Ethan struggled to belong. He tried to fit in with several groups but could not find one that would accept him. He's the type that captivated you the first time you met him. It's easy for Ethan to make new friends, but he struggled to keep them.

In our last friendship group, 'The Brotherhood', Ethan was voted out. He was a misfit and couldn't figure out where he belonged. Ethan played on a local soccer team and always brought down the team's morale. In the last game of a tournament, he was controversially red carded. At the end of the match, he attempted to fight the referee and was suspended for 12 months. Despite all this, he was like a brother. I could confide in him because he was always available. When I was having difficulty in my relationship with Janet, Ethan was there for me.

Ethan was my best friend, and he was a smooth talker and caused drama for the ladies. This guy would rock up to my place each week with a different girl and managed to get them all to be friends with each other. He was the typical player, but it was never a problem for me until I found out that he had started dating Shishi, my niece. As soon as I found out, I confronted Ethan. In response, he burst out emotionally, "I love her, and I have told her everything about my past life. I'm ready to change. I just didn't know how to tell you."

I was enraged. This was my friend. How the hell would he change? I rushed to my niece in an attempt to talk her out of a relationship with Ethan. I was too late. Shishi had fallen head over heels in love with Ethan and there wasn't a thing I could do about it.

I went home feeling angry and guilty that day. If it weren't for me, Shishi may never have met Ethan. Would this be the end of our friendship? Would I be responsible for introducing this hazard to my family if Ethan had not changed as he claimed?

s time went on, Ethan and Shishi's relationship continued to grow stronger and stronger—but not for long. It didn't take long for Shishi to call and confirm my suspicions. She was in tears and mentioned something about a girl calling to tell her Ethan was having sex with her. I was not surprised. I had expected this, after all. I remembered Ethan telling me briefly that a new neighbour had moved in the street a few blokes from his place. I suspected this person was the other woman involved in the supposed affair.

I was torn. Should I be a good uncle and tell Shishi the truth and break her heart? I was not definite that Ethan was cheating with the neighbour, but I suspected some things from the tone of his voice when he told me about this neighbour. Should I be responsible for breaking up the relationship, or say nothing? At this stage, being a good uncle meant either protecting my niece's feelings or telling the truth. I decided not to tell.

Years and years passed, and I am somewhat thankful for not telling the truth at that time. Ethan finally proposed to my niece and promised to spend the rest of his life with her. It was the most incredible feeling ever! My two best friends were finally getting to spend the rest of their lives together! However, deep down, I repeatedly asked myself, *Was Ethan really a changed man?*

And each time, I knew the sad answer.

Can you be an uncle to the bride and the best man to the groom at the same time? Well, I was! I'd been friends with Ethan for so many years, and he couldn't think of anyone else other than me—his brother, best friend and (now) brother-in-law! So, with great joy, I organised a bachelor's night getaway. A famous national destination was scheduled, and the boys set out for a weekend of fun.

On October 6, 2016, Ethan, Chris, me, and three other boys departed together after many years of talking about a boys' trip. It was finally happening, and it felt great. After going to the gym for the past three months, we all looked fit, happy, and very charming. Throughout the trip, we would flirt with almost any girl we set eyes on. It was fun and felt like high school all over again. With the hotel apartment meeting all expectations, the party began while we waited for the other boys to arrive.

On Friday, October 7, the rest of the boys arrived. We were young, black, built, and hungry for fun. But was this too much temptation? Can people really change? Shortly after the night began, we found a street that was full and had all sorts of fun activities. There were six nightclubs on this street, and lots of women: young, middle-aged, black, white, brown—all kinds!

We hit the first club, Bedroom, and the music was slow. There were beds all around the club. The ladies were everywhere. As always, some of the boys took centre stage and began to dance. We all had unique dancing styles, and, as they say, ladies enjoy black boys showing off their dancing talents. Little did they know that not all black men could dance! At this stage, it didn't matter who could and couldn't dance in the group. With all the attention on us, we each grabbed a lady from the crowd and politely danced with them.

The morning after the first night of the weekend getaway, I received a call from my niece. She was crying and told me that Ethan had been tormenting her throughout the night via text messages. I stormed inside Ethan's bedroom, grabbed him, and slammed him on the ground. Before the boys could separate us, I spat out angrily, "You've asked her to marry you. If you ever hurt her, I'll kill you."

When the tension subsided, we talked it over and soon we were back in the moment. To revive the mood, someone suggested we go paintballing and everyone agreed. The 40-minute drive to the place was all about singing and dancing in the cars. Some of the boys would dangerously swap chewing gum from one car to the other while driving parallel at over 100 km/h. It was dangerous and fun!

Once we reached our destination, we stopped the vehicles, but left the engine running so we could continue to blast music while dancing. Everyone wanted to show off. We were a bunch of healthy, fit, young men who wanted to impress.

We took off our shirts and began to dance. Only Ethan was dressed in a pink skirt. The receptionist couldn't help but ask. "You young men look very fine. I would like to take a photo of you all and put it up on the company's Facebook page."

To her dismay, our response was a collective surprise. We had all looked at each other before a loud 'no' was growled. We instantly declined and decided to carry on with our activities. We were seated in a circle, along with the other group of boys that had come to have fun, too. We were divided into separate groups

As soon as we loaded our guns, our group began to walk towards the open space. There were old choppers and tyres—it looked like a combat base with lots of obstacles. Chris immediately raised his weapon behind Ethan, pointed his gun at his head, then slowly moved down his neck, back, and finally, to his bottom.

POW! He shot Ethan's butt at close range. Everyone erupted in laughter as Ethan hopped around in pain. It was a boys thing', and it was Ethan's turn to be humiliated. He was leaving the bachelor's club, after all.

At around 4 pm that same day, we returned to the hotel to freshen up and continue our fun into the night.

On Monday, the weekend was over, and we headed back to Sydney. The wedding took place the weekend that followed. With everything on that day, the short journey in the Hummer from my sister's place, Abbigail, to the park was a dream; we played our music, some drank while others danced all the way there. If there was anything we knew how to do better, it was how to TURN UP!

CHAPTER 21

Finding a Soulmate

Now, let me take you back in time and share a personal story with you. You see, while we were at the hotel, we made a bet to award cash to the first person to bring a girl back. Wallets were full, we were all freshened up, and our confidence was through the roof. At first, it was just a typical night out dancing—I was drinking Red Bull and checking out girls. There was a bit of a scuffle on the dance floor when one of the boys, James, decided to battle another group of boys we met there. After winning the battle, he then attempted to dance with one of the guys' dates! He was punched in the face. All our boys had gotten up to defend him, only to be told by one of the bouncers to either settle down or get thrown out.

It was right after this drama that the most beautiful moment of my life happened. The moment the 24th son spotted the woman who would eventually become, not just his best friend forever, but his soulmate as well. She had beautiful, light-red hair, glowing skin, and a gorgeous smile. She had a unique birthmark above the left side of her lips.

I was captivated from the first moment I saw her. My heart responded immediately, beating faster than normal. My eyes and entire attention were focused on this one shooting star in the club. She was with a friend, and they were having fun, too.

Before I could think twice, I was already making my way towards them. My mind was telling me to stop but my legs kept moving forward until I was right in front of them. This did not go unnoticed by the boys, who already understood the situation. If I wanted to get this girl's full attention, someone needed to provide backup. It was Tim who stepped in to whisk her friend, Samantha, away to the dance floor. It was a clumsy attempt but totally helpful. Tim had been married for six years and had been out of the dating game for a while. In fact, he almost knocked Samantha away with his arm before he could even introduce himself. His actions were really funny to both girls and elicited laughter from Samantha right before they made their way to the dance floor.

With Sam safely out of the way, we had all the privacy we needed for introductions. Her name was Eva. The sweetest sound I had ever heard. As soon as we introduced ourselves, Eva informed me of something. "The club is handing out free pizza!"

I had no idea why she shared that with me, but I immediately blurted out, "Okay then, I will help you search for this mysterious pizza." A minute into the search, I suggested that we go somewhere private so I could get to know more about her. Eva agreed. We ended up heading down to the beach. I was a bit sceptical about asking her about her American accent.

"I am in Australia for a working holiday. I am from Canada," Eva giggled proudly.

Then, more conversations ensued. After that first meeting, we talked every day. Every day for six months.

New Year's Eve was that time of the year that celebrations brought the city's streets to life. We celebrated the new year as a couple for the first time in 2016. Eva and Samantha were in Melbourne, and I was in Sydney. It was 11:50 pm on December 31, 2016, and I was dialling Eva's phone. We could barely hear each other because of the noisy celebrations. At exactly 11:59, I joined the countdown, "Ten, nine, eight, seven, six, five, four, three, two, one! I love you, Eva!"

"I love you too," Eva sobbed.

In that very moment, we both knew we wanted to do this. We wanted to spend the rest of our lives together. I knew exactly the pet name I was going to call her, 'Eve'. The following morning, we started talking about how Eve would tell her family and friends about this guy she had met in Australia. He is black, Muslim, and has a son. Knowing her parents, the two things that worried Eve the most were that her parents would not accept me because of the possibility that she would move to Australia permanently, and, more so, because I had a child.

After an hour of phone calls with her family and friends, the words that stood out from her family the most were, 'Are you dumb?' and from her friends, 'Run.'

Who would blame them? A relationship with a man who lived on the other side of the world, and one who had a child, for that matter, would be unsettling for anyone. It was up to Eve to make her own choice. If she had hoped for support, there was none.

Eve's working visa was in the final period of expiration. She would need to work on a farm for three months if she wanted to stay in Australia for another year. Eve had never worked on a farm before! We spoke on the phone several times discussing how she was going to do this for us.

That day, our conversation had a lot of silent moments. She was mumbling incoherently and choking on her sobs. We both could see the potential of this relationship. It had only been a few months, but we were going strong. Still, was this worth risking everything? What would happen if we didn't work out?

All these questions and more silently hung in the air between us. It remained unuttered, but both of us knew the depth of the consequences Eve's decision would have on us. As we talked, her sniffling continued, and tears threatened to spill from her almond-brown eyes. She had less than 24-hours to make a decision that would change her life forever. By the next day, Eve must decide if she would stay for me or return to Canada.

She was in Melbourne, and I was in Sydney. The very next morning, she Facetimed me. My heart was anxious and nervous as I waited for the answer that I dreaded. Her cheeks were red, her face had a few breakouts, and her eyelids were swollen. She had been crying the whole night and it was very noticeable. It broke me to see her that way.

"Samantha and I will be driving to Sydney first thing tomorrow morning."

And for that one moment, time stopped. Relief

washed over me, and I exhaled a deep breath that I had no idea I had been holding.

That was it. Eve was staying. She loved me enough to put everything on the line. She was choosing to leave all she had ever known to make a new life with me, even though nothing was guaranteed yet. My heart had clutched with emotion as the weight of her sacrifice dawned on me. This woman sure did love me.

At around 6 pm the next day, Samantha and Eve were upstairs at my place doing the final packing and weighing. Samantha was leaving at 8 am the next day. Eve and I were in bed, staring at the ceiling in silence. Though we did not say a word, I felt the emotions she was experiencing, and vice versa. It was like we were somehow communicating through the silence with our thoughts. We remained this way until the beautiful bliss of sleep came. It was already past midnight, and our bodies and mind were tired. It didn't take long for my alarm to ring out softly with the sound of a nature-themed tune. It was time for my daily prayers, and unsteadily, I got up.

Beside me, Eve was still half asleep, her face

drained and exhausted. I took one final look at her before heading to the bathroom to wash up and brush my teeth. After that, I headed downstairs to my corner for prayers. That morning, I let my thoughts wander to Eve's decision to remain in Australia.

Upstairs, the girls were up and finishing some last-minute packing. There was no going back now. Breakfast was quick and simple. In a few minutes, I loaded the car with Samantha's bags, and the girls engaged in a tight, tearful hug.

As I drove to the airport, they sat in the back seat talking about when they would see each other again. We reached the airport and Samantha went to check in. The tears erupted again with a final goodbye now imminent.

As we drove home, Eve reached for my hand and gave me an infectious smile. She slowly leaned over and placed her head on my shoulder. She whispered, "We have a few days together before I leave to go to the farm."

2017 - A New Phase: Life on The Farm

The farm was six hours away from Sydney West in a small town called Barraba.

This day was an exploration day and we decided to spend time in the great outdoors. The sun was rising, and glimpses of sun rays were beaming through the bedroom window as Eve and I got ready for a hike. We had our hiking boots, snacks, and water all packed. Our destination was the Blue Mountains. This was a region with vast natural scenery, hiking spots, lookouts, flora, and fauna. It was the perfect place to spend quality time together outdoors.

We reached the hiking spot at around 8 am. At that time, there weren't many people coming to hike. Eve carried her snacks and water in her pink Canadian backpack, and I held my own bottle as we hiked down the mountain. After an hour and a half of indulging in the finely dispersed droplets of eucalyptus tree oil, we finally reached the bottom of the mountain. I am 5'11", with full chest muscles, broad shoulders, and large overall anatomy. Eve is a 5'5", smaller, and Asian.

We decided to run up the mountain, so I carried Eve's bag and placed my water bottle in it. There were many tourists who were from an Asian background. I was running in front with Eve's bag in my hand, and she was running a few steps behind me. As I was running, I noticed people glaring at me. They turned their heads and looked at Eve for any indication that she was in trouble or needed help. Then they quickly turned their gaze back to me—a big black man running with a girlie pink bag in his hand with a tiny girl running behind him and struggling to catch her next breath. The crowd flowed down the steep, narrow mountain path the same way the rivers met its banks.

The mood of the people swirled like an unseen current beneath the furious dark surface of their faces. In the large crowd of strangers, there wasn't a single smile. Rather, they held an expression of doubt. I was seen as a threat. Without even caring to assess the situation, everyone had simply put their guard up.

First, it had sparked like a start-up campfire, then

it had quickly intensified like a bushfire. At that point, I was already afraid someone was going to tackle, push, or punch me.

Their actions were contagious. Whether they realised it, they all copied each other's actions. Though no one did anything or said anything, but they had growing looks of concern. Maybe people are just scared of black people (ha!). I don't know.

As we were driving back home later that day, I asked Eve what she thought about the situation. "Did you see how your people were looking at me back there? Yeah, everyone was looking at me but didn't say anything."

Eve looked at me with a smile and replied, "Your ass could have been Kung-Fu-ed today." And we both burst out laughing.

The sun was shining bright, and a hot wind was blowing. Eve was packing all sorts of bug sprays and getting ready for the trip to an unknown place—the farm. Soft tunes were playing in the background, and it was like the songs were saying what we felt in our hearts. Our few days together were over, and Eve was heading to the farm, where she would work for three months.

Tears were shed as we exchanged sad goodbyes. Then, she left in her red Toyota Camry. It disappeared as I stood fixed on the side of the road, pondering when I would get to see her again.

Five and a half hours later, it was 8:30 pm and I was playing games to pass the time, secretly waiting to hear from Eve. My heart was anxious just to hear her voice. As if hearing my silent plea, my phone's light slowly came on, and it buzzed like an annoyed rattlesnake.

I rushed to the phone, scooped it up, and waited for a moment to hear her voice. My face immediately lit up in the dark like a star in the sky. Then, the light was quickly extinguished when I heard the sobbing voice through the phone. There were a few seconds of silence. For those seconds, my mind frantically jumped to all the possible worst-case scenarios. I was finally able to force myself to speak. "What happened? You hurt? Where are you?"

The soft, sobbing voice arrived through the phone

like a late Christmas gift. "I am five minutes from the place," Eve said.

"Yeah?" I anxiously replied.

"There were three kangaroos, one big and two small. While I was driving, I saw them too late..."

"Then?"

Eve's voice sounded like a robot. I could only hear every third word. The signal was fading. After two minutes of trying to make out what she was saying, all I got was, "I hit one of them...I think I hit their mother."

"Are you hurt?" I asked frantically. I couldn't hear anything else she was saying after that. I swear I called for the next ten minutes afterwards non-stop.

30 minutes later, I received a call through WhatsApp. It was Eve!

"Are you hurt?"

"No, but those poor baby kangaroos. I hurt their mother..."

It took some time, but I finally managed to convince

Eve to calm down and seek help.

For three months, I visited Eve, and she would come to see me periodically.

One Saturday morning in winter, Chris and I were driving to the Central Coast for a two-hour hike. Among the boys, I used to say being married was like cancer. Worse, it was a prison. You must seek permission to go out or chill with your boys. You even have to ask when to eat and when to go to bed. But recently, I found myself wanting to spend more and more time with Eve without her saying anything. Whenever I was with her, I had this feeling of contentment. She was also unbelievably good with Azlan.

"I want to marry this girl, brother."

We were travelling 110 kilometres an hour on the freeway and Chris was indicating to the left, slowing down before coming to a complete stop. He turned to me with this stupid smile on his face. "Brother, you're in love!" Chris laughed. "I am happy for you, brother!"

Eve returned from the farm the next day. As soon

as she got back, she took charge of activities in the house. She was in my kitchen wearing grey shorts with pictures of the yellow bear with the red shirt named Pooh, a black singlet, and blue gloves. She put bleach in a bucket and used a sponge to scrub years of stains off the kitchen walls. She would be living with me for a month before flying to Canada to face her family. She was going to tell them of her plans to move thousands of kilometres across the world and start a relationship with a man who has a child. And of course, someone who prays five times every day and eats halal! Oh, and someone who isn't a successful Asian man, either. When I say not successful, I mean that I'm not a doctor, engineer, or lawyer.

Eva's wants and perceptions diverged immensely from her parents'. A lot was at stake for her parents, and they dreaded the thought of having their daughter move across the world.

When it comes to marriage, the idea of coupling has been embedded in us from childhood. The desire to have another, and sometimes the thoughts of being a prince or princess just for one day, thrives on the desire to get married. For me, I just couldn't imagine my life without my best friend in it! I have never trusted anyone in my life other than my only mentor, my mother. My mother will always be my mother, but I felt safe and had no hesitation sharing my thoughts and ambitions with Eve. I knew what I had to do next.

I texted Eva's brothers, Andres and Victor, who I had built a relationship with over the past months and told them of my plans to call their parents to ask for their blessings. I was going to ask Eve to marry me. Eve's parents speak English, but they would require an interpreter for my thick accent, so Victor volunteered to go to his parents' home to translate for them. People around me have always said I am a positive and confident person, but picture a toddler trying to talk—that was me trying to ask for Eve's parents' blessing.

After about 30 minutes of being interviewed, they said YES!

CHAPTER 22

The Proposal

I planned to do the proposal in British Columbia's most breathtaking popular hiking spot. It had majestic glacier-laden peaks towering high above and was only a two-and-a-half-hour drive from Vancouver. The three glacier lakes turned Joffre lakes' moderate hike into an incredible, beautiful natural art.

Eve was travelling to Canada in a few days, and she had no idea of my plans. Eve had already travelled to

Canada at this point. I would join her the next day, unknown to her, or so I thought. The plan was that Victor, her brother, who had not done any hiking or engaged in physical activities in forever, would pick me up from the airport, drive us two-and-a-half hours to the provincial park, and hike up with me. Andres, on the other end, would start the hike with Eve precisely 30 minutes after us.

To have a pleasant morning, I decided to go to bed early. I was lying on my bed thinking about the most significant decision in my life and my eyes were slowly closing...

I am back in Sierra Leone, and I am ten years old again.

The war is nearing its end now, but the rebels still visit different towns periodically. Some people are still cautious about the possibility of a rebel attack, so they continue to hide in the nearby forest. My family and a few other families decide to come back to the town for a few hours after years of running back and forth from the village to the forest. We hope the rebels won't visit our village during this time.

The front yard has a mango tree and I decide to climb it. I pick the mangos and eat them up the tree. My mother and stepfather go back to the forest to the palm tree hideout house to collect the rest of our possessions. For the past three months, we spent our time at the hideout house. There are no toilets. Children are not allowed to play because of the fear of noise. We hunt and fish for food. When we catch anything from hunting or fishing, we cook it over the wood fire with no cooking ingredients, just salt, if we were lucky to find some.

After being up the mango tree for hours, I decide to fall asleep up there, not knowing that the rebels have arrived and that everyone has run back to the forest for safety. The rebels' noise wakes me. From the tree, I see them dancing. They hold their guns up while the captured female cooks for them. Hours later, some of the rebels debate about whether they want mangoes or not. My trembling heart beats even harder. I desperately pray that, in the end, they decide against eating mangoes.

Then, I hear a commanding voice say, "I want fresh mangoes." It is their leader. This is it. My fate is sealed. The rebels walk towards the mango tree. They see me suspended high in the air.

I start to cry, pleading for my life in the process.

"I am sorry...I am very sorry..."

I don't even know what I am sorry for, but that is the only thing that I can think to say. The smallest among them, not much older than me, points his gun at me and opts to shoot me, but the other suggests that I pick the mangoes for them first. They would decide what to do with me after that.

Temporarily spared, I move from branch to branch and pick the fresh mangoes. I do not want to stop because that might just be my last moment.

"Enough! Get down," they tell me. They tie my hands behind my back and stand me up in front of hundreds of rebels. Everyone yells their preferred method of torture. Finally, one claims to have magic. He says he will cut off my penis and balls, and then he will use magic to put everything back in position without me dying. I am drenched in sweat, hoping someone will talk sense into him. I hope they just shoot me instead. That will be better, *I think to myself.*

But nobody does. If anything, they seem excited by his proposal. The hundreds of rebels chant, "Magic! Magic! Magic!"

"Before you do this, I-I have one request. I want to-I want to pray." This is my last desperate attempt. I will do anything to prolong this madness.

"Prayers won't save you today, but knock yourself out," the self-proclaimed magician mocks. He gets ready while I stand there and pray to delay the process.

"It is time! Behold, everyone," the magician yells. You could hear a pin drop. The whole place is silent. Everyone leans forward to get a clear view of this so-called magic. He takes out two knives, but neither are sharpened.

"Sorry, boy. I haven't got a sharp one today, so this process might be painful for you," he whispers to me, "but lots of fun for my friends here."

My pants are coming off. Someone behind me removes them. I stand there naked. This strange man holds my private parts together as I struggle against the other rebels who hold me in a firm grip.

He raises the knife for one final chant, then he lowers his arm to begin the process.

"No! No!"

I jumped out of bed, saturated in sweat, disorientated, and panicked. Where am I? I touched my whole body and ran to the bathroom to check my penis.

Sigh. What a relief! I had been dreaming again!

It was the day I planned to fly to Canada to ask Eve to marry me. The ring was ready, and I was taken back to my childhood in my sleep. This always happens when I am about to make a big decision. I was going to ask this girl, who I had only been dating for a handful of months, to marry me. In fact, just having the thought of asking anyone to marry me was the most shocking thought ever. But here I was, on the train, and soon enough on a fish in the air, heading to Vancouver, Canada.

Throughout the 15-hour flight, I did not close my eyes for a wink. I was afraid that I'd be taken back to my childhood and the thought of never waking up from

The 24th Son

my sleep prevented me from shutting my eyes.

I arrived at the airport at 7:31 am. Vancouver was delivering the sweetest, cool morning weather (19 degrees Celsius) of the year. There was beautiful sunshine and less humidity than many other cities in Canada.

It was 8:30 am and Victor wasn't at the airport yet.

Was he not coming? Was this all a joke? Thoughts were screaming in my head. Finally, at 9:03 am, a blue Toyota pulled up and a gentle-looking man leaned out of the window. "Hi, I'm Victor. Sorry I was late. How was your flight?"

"Good, thanks for doing this."

"Sure! Do you want to drive? I am still waking up," Victor asked.

"Uhh, okay."

In Vancouver, they drove on the right side of the road. In Australia, we drive on the left side. After two-and-a-half hours of driving, we made it! I grabbed a jacket and hiking boots from my bag, and off we went to the trail. The pace was slower than I'd normally go, but I acknowledged the great challenge it was for Victor.

We reached the first lake, and it was mind-blowing; just like all the stories I had heard. But I did not want to do it there. "The next one will be even better," I said to myself. So, we continued to the second one. The trail was becoming steeper and more challenging. We reached the turquoise water. Eve had told me earlier that the water's colour was actually blue, but I still saw it as green.

All three lakes were located on the same trail. The second one was like an imaginary picture of heaven. It was like nothing I had ever seen before. The stunning, striking suspense in the water and the reflection of the blue and green wavelength of sunlight was breathtaking and only further heightened my anticipation for the third lake. I could not wait to see it.

We continued hiking along the trail and then, just a few minutes later, we saw it. The majestic third lake in all its glory. And yes, it had everything the second lake had, but better. The snow on the mountain across the water gave me a flash of November 2005 during my journey to the land of hope when I had seen snow for the first time in my life.

This was it! This was where I was going to ask her to marry me. It was a special and beautiful spot. Just perfect for the beautiful soul I wanted to spend my life with.

While he was still catching his breath, Victor began to dutifully set the camera up. I was standing on the rock closest to the water. I had attempted to stand in the water earlier, but it was mission impossible. My body had started shutting down in about three seconds. This was glacial water we were talking about and only the snow queen could dare stand in this water for longer.

Just behind us, oblivious to what was ahead of her, I could hear Eve laughing at Andres dying from the hike. Just as she reached the clearing that ended the trail and joined the third lake, she raised her gaze and saw me standing there.

I had imagined this moment. Her eyes would shoot wide with surprise and the tears would run down her face. Next, she would rush over to me and squeeze my big frame into her tiny arms. Her reaction was just as I had imagined it and more.

"What are you doing here?" she said, trying to keep the sobs from choking her.

She was hitting me on the chest, and she poked further. After that, I was not in control of the words that came out of my mouth. I was shaking, cold, and tired with a little bit of adrenaline in the tank. I said words along the lines of, "Thank you for travelling across the world to the land down under and allowing me to find you. I never thought I would ever think of asking anyone to marry me, but you forced me by just being the incredible person you are. I love you." I went down on one knee after finding a stable rock. I asked her to marry me, and SHE SAID YES!

Little did I know that the proposal, which was supposed to be a surprise, was not a surprise to Eva. Eve had her suspicions. She told me that when she was packing some clothes that she bought me from the outlet stores, her mother came into her room and told her not to pack them yet. To make things worse, her father joined in the conversation and asked, "When is your boyfriend coming?" Her mother's eyes popped out of their sockets, and she quickly turned to slap her husband on the chest as a signal to not say any more.

Another occurrence that raised suspicions was that her brother, Andres, had asked her to go on a hike. Andres was not one to enjoy the great outdoors or too much physical activity. She told me how it was strange for Andres to ask her to go on a hike with him. Nervously, I told her to wear some make-up to go on the hike so she could take some nice photos with her brother. To add to all of this, since Victor was late in picking me up from the airport, Andres had to stall her. He had convinced Eve to go for breakfast with him at a local restaurant, despite the fact that she had already had something to eat.

Lastly, I was a terrible liar. Eve had called me when I was at the Sydney airport. She asked me where I was. I told her, "I'm at the airport for work with my client. I won't be able to answer the phone for a while." This confirmed that her suspicions were correct. She had googled flights from Sydney to Vancouver and had timed how long I would be away from my phone.

On our final day in Vancouver, we visited several venues. We saw a lake in Burnaby, BC and noticed it had a restaurant and an outdoor tent for weddings. Without a doubt, we both knew this was what we wanted. We booked a date for the wedding: Sunday, August 2nd, 2020. Afterwards, we travelled together back to Sydney.

We started to make wedding preparations. We had booked a photographer, videographer, florist, a hair and make-up team, and a DJ. We had friends help gather some ideas for décor, such as wine bottles, wood slices, and the wedding arch. Unfortunately, after all that preparation, we heard about the coronavirus. We didn't think much of it at first, as it had not reached Canada or Australia.

Eventually, we had our first Covid-19 case in Sydney and lockdowns were put in place. We realised the seriousness of the situation and contacted our wedding venue to see what our options were. We made the decision to postpone the wedding another year, to August 2021.

Since I arrived in Australia, I had dreamed of

becoming a homeowner. Eve and I decided to use the money we had saved for our wedding and, with the help from my mother and Eve's parents, we purchased our first home! We went with a home and land package and needed to wait for the land to register and the construction to start. My mother had visited my homeland before the pandemic started and was stuck in Sierra Leone. Flights were limited and so were our funds.

My mother had fallen very ill and had run out of her daily prescription medications. We were worried that she would not get the proper care she needed.

In early 2021, we saw that circumstances of the pandemic had worsened, and we could not foresee a date when travel would be possible, so we cancelled the Canada wedding altogether.

My mother was still on the other side of the globe, and we knew that we had to do something. We had spent the last of our savings on our new home. With the help of other family members, we gathered enough funds to purchase a ticket for my mother's flight home. Finally, my mother returned to Australia and received proper treatments at the hospital. When she recovered, she visited our brand-new home. She broke down in tears and could not stop thanking God.

We decided that we wanted to have children, but Eve did not want to start trying until after we were married. There were talks of the international borders opening in June, so we decided to plan a small wedding in our backyard for June. As June came closer, there were talks of border openings being pushed until November. We changed our minds once again and moved the date to November 27, 2021.

On November 1st, 2021, Australia's borders opened to Australian residents and their immediate family. This meant parents, spouses, and children who were double vaccinated could apply for a travel exemption to enter the country.

The issue that we had was that Canada had given the choice for people to get mixed-dose vaccinations, which were not accepted by the Australian government. Days later, news had been released that mixed-dose vaccinations were accepted in Australia. Eve wasted no time and applied for travel exemptions for both her parents, which were approved in about a week. She convinced her parents to make last-minute arrangements with her father's workplace to allow him to take leave. Eve applied for their visas, and everything was in place. We got to celebrate our special day with our friends and family.

My mom had now witnessed the three largest milestones of my life: graduating with a bachelor's degree from a well-known university, owning a brand-new home, and marrying the love of my life!

CHAPTER 23

The War Versus Me

Any moment could trigger memories of the past taking me back to my childhood. This time, it happened while driving.

Eva and I were going on a small trip to a camping spot in Honeymoon Bay, part of Jervis Bay. It was approximately ten km from the edge of Currong, along the point perpendicular to Lighthouse Road.

Honeymoon Bay is a small, sheltered bay located

south of Sydney. It is a perfect spot to spend time near the beach. The camping spot was fully booked out for the summer holiday period via a ballot system.

It was 9:48 pm on Friday, November 22, 2019. My hands were firmly placed on the wheel as I drove to this long-awaited, heaven on earth camping site. While driving, as I looked in the rear-view mirror of my car and saw pitch black behind me, I was teleported back to Sierra Leone. I was taken back to when my family and I were running away from the rebels.

It is a dark, rainy night. The night we have to run for our lives from the rebels. We are going to sleep but we have our ears pressed flat on the ground, as we were advised, so we can hear any footsteps. We have only as much as a five-second reaction time between life and death.

The place is dark as blackness itself and we must run away, as far from the roads as possible. Our only concern is the rebels. Snakes and other wild animals are the least of our worries.

It is sad, but these life and death situations are becoming fun, in a different type of way. During these times, all we are thinking about is how to survive the night and not get killed by the rebels or wildlife. After so long, it becomes a routine—it is something we look forward to as a child. It is our own version of the Squid Game, only there is no prize—well, except your life.

This is one of many nights my parents will stay awake. They take turns and are vigilant about any noise. Their hearing is so powerful now that they can hear footsteps, or any type of noise, from a mile away. The only words we need to listen for are 'they are coming'. Despite how deep you are in your sleep, you have five seconds to wake up, wake anyone around you, and run to the forest.

Tonight is one such night. We run into the bush with one of the young men, George, from the village, who has not slept for days. During the day, he hunts and fishes for the family. I have the flu this week. After running into the forest tonight, we both fall asleep at the campsite almost instantly. Out of extreme exhaustion, and my blocked nose, George and I snore. Diamond wakes us and tells us that the two oldest people in our group have decided to hide elsewhere. They look at each other and start packing their sleeping items. They say, "We are not going to get killed because of these two idiots. We are going somewhere else."

Apparently, our snores are loud. Everyone bursts into laughter as the two men state their reasons for leaving the group. These men are around 70 years of age. They are the two eldest here, yet they are the most afraid of dying. At night, we change locations multiple times and go further into the bush. This time, I can't sleep due to the fear of snoring again. Besides, having an hour of sleep is a privilege that rarely came.

Eve leaned over to kiss me on the cheek, and I was jolted back to the present.

"Are you okay? You looked to be in deep thought."

"Yes," I quickly replied.

Soon, we arrived at the front gate of our camping site at Jervis Bay. I know it's sad, but some part of me felt nostalgic after remembering that life and death situation. I was missing it, in a different type of way.

Monday, March 16, 2020.

As I write this, the world is battling the terrible Covid-19 pandemic. I am still battling not just the pandemic, but my personal nightmares and trauma of the civil war. That means a triple struggle for me. Every little thing could take me back these days. I no longer need to shut my eyes for the nightmares to come. I could be wide awake and still be taken back to those traumatic memories.

One fateful Monday on March 16, 2020, at 4:30 pm, I was sitting in my office looking outside my office window. It was a cloudy 23-degree day.

As I stared outside, I saw a middle-aged, 5'9" tall lady with long, blonde hair walk across the street. She was holding a Coles brand pack of 24-roll toilet paper labelled with a $10 sticker. My heart began to beat fast as blood rushed to my limbs, fuelling action just like when I was seven years old.

I was sweating and my feet were shaking. Why this was happening, I knew not. All I know is that I quickly disconnected my laptop, put it in my work bag, grabbed my jacket, phone, and keys, and rushed down the stairs. I went down the narrow hallway, down another set of stairs, and then out the front door of my office building.

Almost robotic-like, I turned right, walked for two minutes into the red and white Coles fuel station, and grabbed one pack of 24-roll toilet paper for $10! As I stepped outside the fuel station, it finally hit me on my face. The street that was usually packed with cars was empty. The gym next door to my work that was always packed with seniors and fitness gurus was also empty! As I continued walking up the hill to the rooftop car park, my body hairs suddenly rose from my arms down to my calves.

A cold wind is blowing. As I look up at the cloudy sky, I am suddenly a seven-year-old boy. That seven-year-old boy in the village during the war occasionally visits the town. How cold and dark it used to be.

Reflecting back as a 30-year-old man to that seven-year-old boy, the world is full of worries, and rightly so. Covid-19 created uncertainty in the world, so much so that even toilet paper has become the new gold. I am unfazed. I see everyone around me worrying, but I am just grateful I didn't die 23 years ago. The nightmares and the trauma of the civil war had prepared me for this moment.

Then, I returned to reality. I had been wandering in my thoughts again. In my daydreams. I had no recollection of how I managed to reach my car, nor do I remember how I drove on the highway.

"Calm down...focus!" I chided myself. So, I continued driving home and made sure that I kept my concentration, lest I lost focus on the highway.

When I got home, I placed the toilet paper on top of the coffee table. An hour later, my beautiful, unmaterialistic fiancée arrived home from work. As she was putting her keys down, she glanced over at the new gold, and she screamed with pure delight.

Instantly, she ran towards me, jumped into my arms, and kissed me relentlessly. "I have toilet paper," she sang happily. The toilet paper was for her, not for me. She is not a social media person; she only checks her Instagram two or three minutes a day. Surprisingly, she reached into her bag, got her phone, took a picture of the toilet paper, and shared it on her story. She captioned the picture: "Came home to meet 24-rolls of toilet paper, so romantic!"

I thought to myself, it is time I shared one of the many colourful stories of my past with her. So later that night, as we started our before-bed conversation, I told her I had something on my mind. "I want to share with you an experience. Here we are celebrating toilet paper. Today, I was taken back to when I was a boy, and one of the things that played in my mind was when we had no toilets in the village..."

Eve giggled at my description, but I was only getting started. "When I needed to poop, I'd run a kilometre into the bush and poop on the ground, and sometimes, you'd see dry poops around. You know what I used as toilet paper?"

"No...what?"

"Leaves...beautiful green leaves," I laughed. "I used leaves to wipe my bottom, and you know what?"

"What?"

"Sometimes, my fingers would accidentally poke a

hole through the leaf in the attempt to clean myself properly, and I'd end up with poop on my fingers."

"Ewww...gross!"

She was grossed out, and I smiled in response.

For many years, people would ask me about my personal journey and what it felt like during the war. I have never been able to explain it in a way that people understand it. The cancellation of our wedding, the disparaging fear across the world, and the uncertainties caused by Covid-19 was the only situation that gave me a glimmer of hope as a comparison. It is something I can use now when I try to explain some of my personal war nightmares.

CHAPTER 24

I am not Suffering

The white bed sheets on my side of the bed were turning yellow. Today, I came from work to hear, "New sheets!" as I walked into our bedroom.

I walked up the stairs feeling the warm, extremely comfortable, dark-grey carpet under my strong feet. I walked into the bedroom where Eve had changed the bed sheets and pillowcases. They were now blue.

Every night, I travelled somewhere I'm not always

familiar with. An ocean of nightmares where I always have to try and survive or save someone I love. One thing I knew for sure was that I always woke up saturated and disoriented. It was never a pleasant sight.

Now, most times, I do not even remember where I am when I wake up. According to Eve, being in my arms when sleeping is the safest place on Earth for her. Now, my beautiful, clingy partner would always attempt to touch me, first my legs, but by the time she reached my chest, her hands were wet.

I always smile when I wake up during the night and tell her I am exercising in my sleep. That is the reason I have a six-pack with minimal gym sessions and can eat anything and never gain weight. Ha—working on those jokes again.

On a serious note, I am striving to hide this from my family and hoping to solve the situation on my own. When putting Azlan to bed in recent months, I am careful not to fall asleep in his bed because I'm afraid it would become saturated with sweat. The nightmares are like a horse that carry me home after I have explored the dark.

Going for long drives on the highway with my sports car, my favourite music on, and the windows down is the only therapy I know. It releases the pressure in my head. But every time I go for a drive, my wife worries about whether she will ever see me again. That was because of an incident two months ago.

One bright winter morning, the sun lashed against my rapid red Ford Mustang's windscreen and my face as I drove with my windows down on the West Link M7 tolled urban motorway in Sydney, Australia— formerly known as the Sydney Orbital. I drove a little over the speed limit going southbound. My vision started to go blurry a few minutes into the ride. For how long, I am not sure.

I am back in the village as that little skinny boy with the dry white snot splashed on my cheeks. I'm wearing a big smile. I run through the green corn farm near the town with the little girls that have the beautiful butterfly dresses. Everyone is giggling. This is what it is like when we are not running away from the rebels.

I felt my wheels bumping over the highway lane

dividers, but I kept the car steady. I peered down the empty road. Soon enough, I returned to that beautiful place I was a moment ago.

The difference this time is that the village is pitch black, with no sign of light. There isn't even a single star in the night sky. There is only complete silence. I am standing in the middle of the town under the torrents of rain frantically looking left, right, up, and down...the town is empty!

I hear the sounds of gunshots in the distance. My heart rate increases even more. My forearm thrashes my face like a windshield wiper. It goes back and forth, attempting to clear the rapid drops of rain and tears that have somehow mixed together. Yet, it seems like my arms are not moving fast enough.

There are 16 torchlights suddenly blazing in front of me, piercing through this impenetrable darkness. With a jolt, I realise these are people walking towards me. Fear grips me intensely, paralysing my feet firmly to the ground.

Again, I heard my wheels bumping over the highway lane dividers, together with a loud overhead horn. It was a truck! Without thinking, I swerved into the other lane. My car was in the middle lane, and there were trucks in both the right and left lanes. There were cars in front and behind me. I had no room.

Then, it happened. I slammed on the brakes, and Ely, which was what I had nicknamed my car, spun into the left lane, and crushed itself against the double front tyres of a huge, yellow truck. The passenger door window shattered, interrupting and saving me from the darkness I was in. As my vision cleared, I was already squeezed in between two trucks and was losing control of Ely. Images of my brother, Musa, Father, and Samba flashed in my mind like a repeating slideshow. The last thing I heard was one final loud sound. *Boom!*

Suddenly, all I felt was a heavy weight, like a mountain, on top of my chest. It was pushing the air from my lungs. It was the last thing I remember before the bliss of darkness welcomed me as Ely spun out of my control.

Is this the end? Did I survive this much only to lose it still? constantly battling a war within myself? And what—just what—did I need to truly be free?

In the hardest of times, you can choose to see things in a positive way. I prefer to see my childhood trauma as a positive. Without that trauma, I would not have been able to migrate to Australia, which, to me, is one of the best countries in the world.

It is too late to give up on my quest. I will survive anything! I will not give up. I am Ibrahim Bangura— the 24th Son.

Epilogue

Shishi, my annoying and gorgeous niece, was on the phone with me.

My hands were shaking. My big, red lips trembled. My eyes were full of tears.

"I don't know. I'm not sick. I do not have a vision pro-problem," I stuttered.

I was barely able to get the words out. Shishi was sobbing on the other end.

My great-grandfathers had done well in giving me the genes I had. I was rarely sick and had no hereditary problems.

"Wha-What could this be? What is happening to me, Shishi?"

There was a brief silence on her end before she spoke again. This time, her words were grave and foreboding. "Home," she said. "I-I think you need to go back home to see your brother's and father's graves. But, most importantly, you need to face your fear of the place that haunts you in your nightmares. The place that turns everything around you to darkness each time the memories come."

"Home?"

"Yes. Maybe you've been fighting the wrong battle all along. Maybe it's time to confront this darkness to get closure."

And then it dawned on me. The war might be over, but my battle is far from won. If anything, my survival is threatened by the very past I have struggled to escape.

The story of the 24th son is far from over. There are several incomplete pieces of the puzzle that must be addressed. If anything, this story is merely the beginning and only one piece of the puzzle. To truly survive this threat, I must revisit each piece—each story one by one until the puzzle is complete.

What piece will I find next? I had a total of 23 siblings. Whose story will I revisit next? What will I find on this new journey? And, most importantly, which piece will help me find closure?

Perhaps I should ask my mother....

Acknowledgement

This book has over a decade in the making and would not have been possible without the amazing group of family, friends, and colleagues I have been so fortunate to call my team.

First and foremost, I would like to thank Allah for giving me the wisdom and will to see this project through. I would like to acknowledge and express my gratitude to my father, Santigie Bangura, my mother, Marie Bangura, and Elder mama, Sento Bangura, for their sacrifices in raising my siblings and me.

I wish to show my appreciation to my sister, Salamatu Bangura, for encouraging me to start putting my thoughts down and for believing in me.

To my sister, Abie Kallay, who supported me in migrating to Australia.

A special thanks to my wife, Eva Truong Bangura, for listening to my crazy ideas, day and night, supporting me with grammar, and believing in me.

I want to extend my special gratitude to Kadiatu Shishi Bangura for helping me generate ideas and with the spelling of difficult native words.

I wish to extend my special thanks to Susan McInnes for reviewing my first drafts and providing valuable feedback and encouragement.

To Nimish Samudra for having unweary belief in me. For supporting me in finessing my craft and reaching out to schools and local multicultural centres to give back to my community.

I would like to thank JB Favour, Lily Lindon from The Novelry, and Hailey for helping me edit my book.

About the Author

I have survived so much trauma and have felt compelled to tell it, in a way that is raw and yet has so much humour and empathy.

I moved to Australia in 2005 as a refugee from Medina, Sierra Leone, West Africa. I attended an intensive English school, followed by year 11 and 12 at Wyndham College (Senior High School). Furthermore, I am an alumnus of the University of Western Sydney (Parramatta). I graduated with a degree in Bachelor of Business and Commerce in 2015.

My education background in Bachelor of Business and Commerce specialising in Management and

Human Resources, together with my qualification in disability services, was inspired by my personal experience with my brother. It provided me with knowledge on ways to provide individualised support to the people with disabilities.

My experience with vulnerable people started at the age of nine when I cared for my disabled brother. When I migrated to Australia, I transferred my personal experiences with my brother to a Support Worker, Team Leader, Client Service Manager and Regional Manager role in Accommodation Support and Shared Living Arrangements.

www.ingramcontent.com/pod-product-compliance
Lightning Source LLC
Chambersburg PA
CBHW031933090426
42811CB00002B/171